Moving from a Life of Success
To a Life of Significance

Carl Youngberg outlines hands-on tools to conquer fear and clarify strengths. Simply put, this book is an investment in your future. I found this book to be fun to read, straightforward and immensely practical.

Vince Poscente
New York Times Bestselling Author
Speaker Hall of Fame and Olympian

As a volunteer in the Peace Corps to his phenomenal career in retail as a Buyer and Educator for Neiman-Marcus and Saks Fifth Avenue, to his incredibly successful career as a corporate speaker, facilitator and coach, Carl Youngberg models what he has written about in his book. He has truly made himself matter to thousands of people and teaches his readers to refuse to be ruled by fear. His message is a message of bravery and courage...courage to **Make Yourself Matter.**

Jane Handly, MA, CPAE, Speaker's Hall of Fame
Author of *Why Women Worry*
and *The Lifeplus Program for Getting Unstuck*

Carl Youngberg puts his finger right on the key to helping individuals grow in the work they do. When people make the difference in their organizations everyone benefits. By giving readers the "how" of **Make Yourself Matter,** *he shows the path to becoming indispensable.*

Tony Jeary
Author of *Life is A Series of Presentations*
And *Success Acceleration*

*I firmly believe that people who are willing to engage--get engaged (as well as hired, well paid and they have more friends). Carl Youngberg's awesome book, **Make Yourself Matter**, is The Field Guide to True Workplace Engagement. This book is key to establishing relationships at work that work. Read it, live it, and progress.*

Dean Lindsay
Author of *The Progress Principle* and *Cracking the Networking CODE: 4 Steps to Priceless Business Relationships*

Carl takes us on a journey we want to take...the one that seeks out and identifies our strengths. Enjoy and learn from the journey...I did!

Al Lucia, Speaker, Author and Consultant
America's Lifeline to the People Side of Business and author of *Walk the Talk: And Get the Results You Want*

Robin —

Make Yourself Matter™
Become Your Own Best Asset

You are
terrific
Carl

2009

Make

Yourself

Matter

Become Your Own Best Asset

By **Carl D. Youngberg**

Speaker, Author, Coach

Published By

ExpertsThatSpeak.com Publishing

Richardson, Texas 75080

For information or book ordering:
www.ExpertsthatSpeak.com
214-227-9916   David@ExpertsThatSpeak.com

First Edition, First Printing 2007
Second Edition, First Printing January 2008
Third Edition, First Printing May 2008

Credits
Author photos by Terry Cockerham
Cover Design by Willie Baronet
Edited by Judy Hoffman and Kate Sullivan

Contents

Foreword

By
Mark LeBlanc

Every once in a while, God winks at you and puts a very special person in your way. How lucky am I that I have had a chance to meet, know, and learn from someone like Carl.

Traveling the world, I have met and spoken to literally thousands of people. I can count on a couple of hands the people that have made a significant difference in my life, and Carl is one of those special people I can truly count on as a friend and confidante.

In his own life, Carl has made a regular practice of turning fear into potential and anxiety into achievement. As a professional speaker and coach, he has shared with thousands the basis for fear and in this book, he helps us understand and discover how to use it to our advantage.

Most people know what to do. But, they allow fear to paralyze them from taking action in the direction of their dreams. Here, Carl outlines strategies and ideas for stepping up to the plate, and standing out from the crowd. He laces it with a unique blend of wisdom that will touch your heart, engage your mind, and stir your soul.

Yes, you can do this. And you now have Carl on your team. If you allow the simple truths that he writes about to become part of your thinking and your actions, you will be richer for the experience. And you will make yourself matter in ways that amaze you.

Read this book, again and again. Make it your desktop or bedside companion, and refer to it often. Let this be the dividing line in the sand and you will embark on a journey filled with grace, honor, and respect

Respect for others. But, most of all, respect for you. Go make yourself matter. Because you do.

Mark LeBlanc
Author of *Growing Your Business When YOU are The Business!*
2007-2008 President, National Speakers Association

In the beginning, there was fear

When the phone rang, I was pounding on the keyboard trying to pull together a plan for the next quarter.

"Can I see you in my office in 15 minutes?" My stomach lurches like the final flight approach into Hong Kong. My mouth turns as dry as the Sahara and my life at work parades before my eyes like last rites.

"Will I be fired, caught, demoted, moved, or just maybe, even...congratulated?"

What we experience is the common physiological response to a fear-based situation. While it kept us safe living in caves where fight or flight meant life, death or injury, today we have the same reactions but to different stimuli.

We react to corporate tigers in boardrooms and faceless accountants who can change our lives with a single keystroke. It is fear, and our lives can be filled with it.

This book is dedicated to fighting fear, to getting unstuck and to building yourself into your biggest asset.

You will learn how to *Make Yourself Matter* using the assets you already own. This book is all you have to buy, but it is not all you have to do. Your action is key.

Using just one of these simple truths can propel you from being a business expense to a business essential. You will become indispensable and possibly unforgettable.

Be the kind of person everyone remembers and everyone values!

In a typical career, whether you're competing for a job, a sale, a contract, a client or anything else you value, **there's nothing more critical to your success than your ability to stand out.** As a uniquely qualified, valuable, appealing individual, we want to be someone who other people want to work with, work for, know and help. When we enter a room, we like to be noticed and known for the abilities and talents for what we do well.

Nothing will set you apart, make people notice and remember you, and get you recognized like the unmistakable qualities that make you matter. <u>Make yourself matter people are a highly valued commodity</u>. They can be spotted right away. And you always remember them.

While much of this book's focus will be on the workplace, people who matter don't lose that quality when they leave the job every evening. I have found many people who matter frequently avoid excess stress because they tend to be the same person, whether on the job, or at home with their family and their community.

Dan Wilson, an executive coach and successful former municipal bonds trader writes frequently about the people and places he has known. In his recent essay series, *Abundant Living*, he captures the essence of *Make Yourself Matter* in his remembrance of Rookh Richards, his elderly good friend who lived a block away from him growing up in his hometown of Paducah, Texas.

Did you ever know someone like that who you were always excited to see? Rookh was one of those people. She had a great attraction about her, the kind that comes from a spirit of humor, warmth and generosity.

Sometime during my high school years, Rookh's health failed and she passed away. I recall sitting at the funeral mourning the loss of my friend, yet remembering the excitement I had felt when I would see her down the street headed my way.

What do people think about me, I sometimes wonder, when they see me headed their way? Have I touched someone's life like Rookh did mine?

I have found that people like Rookh and many others I have encountered live lives that matter. Julia Child said, "Life itself is the proper binge." People who live life enthusiastically and with gusto and connect with other people are the reasons I wrote the book. From them, I realized there was another way of living and thinking so different than my own experience.

Personal development is a marriage - not a fling

People who have attended my speeches and workshops have told me that these truths become a challenge to both own and maintain. What I present are not easy truths and far from a flavor of the month.

To live them requires discipline, devotion and above all, willingness. Effective personal development is a marriage, not a fling.

This is the story of *Make Yourself Matter*. It's an idea born over Caesar salad with friends that has become a critical conversation and has grown to bigger discussions, a keynote speech and now a book.

It is also the story of how input -- from friends and strangers both here and all over the world has been incorporated in these thoughts and enriches the dialogue.

Living a life that matters doesn't happen by accident. It's not a matter of circumstance but of choice.

Not everything that matters can be counted and not everything that can be counted matters.

- Albert Einstein

Acknowledgements

To those I love:

Your unconditional love has transformed me and made this work possible.

Thank you:

Laura, my daughter, said "Daddy, you are a natural storyteller like Garrison Keillor on Prairie Home Companion -- go tell your stories."

Jane Handly heard me speaking at Neiman Marcus and told me to become a speaker.

Kelly Hewitt made me sign a pledge to get the book written.

David McNair simply said "let me help."

Judy Hoffman owns a red editing pencil, and I gave her lots of chances to use it. And enough other people to fill the Manhattan phone directory. You know who you are, but this is a small book.

The meeting of two personalities is like the contact of two chemical substances: if there is any reaction, both are transformed.

- Carl Jung (1875 - 1961)

Live A Life That Matters

Ready or not, someday it will all come to an end

There will be no more sunrises, no minutes, hours, or days.

All the things you collected, whether treasured or forgotten, will pass to someone else.

Your wealth, fame, and temporal power will shrivel to irrelevance.

It will not matter what you owned or what you were owed.

Your grudges, resentments, frustrations, and jealousies will finally disappear.

So, too, your hopes, ambitions, plans, and to-do lists will expire.

The wins and losses that once seemed so important will fade away.

It won't matter where you came from, or on what side of the tracks you lived, at the end.

It won't matter whether you were beautiful or brilliant.

Even your gender and skin color will be irrelevant.

So what will matter? How will the value of your days be measured?

What will matter is not what you bought, but what you built; not what you got, but what you gave.

What will matter is not your success, but your significance.

What will matter is not what you learned, but what you taught.

What will matter is every act of integrity, compassion, courage or sacrifice that enriched, empowered or encouraged others to emulate your example.

What will matter is not your competence, but your character.

What will matter is not how many people you knew, but how many will feel a lasting loss when you're gone.

What will matter are not your memories, but the memories that live in those who loved you.

What will matter is how long you will be remembered, by whom and for what.

- Author Unknown

Introduction

Discover the 10 Simple Truths to
Make Yourself Matter
today!

This simple formula is one I used throughout my career:
*   1) Build expertise*
*   2) Get people to recognize it*

- Keith Ferrazzi - author and speaker

Life is calling. How will you answer?

- Carl Youngberg

What's a Caesar Salad got to do with it anyway?

The waiter brought our crisp salads to the blonde wood table and with a perfunctory *"Do you need anything else?"* departed. But we hardly noticed as we were deep in a conversation more important to us than romaine lettuce. I was enjoying my favorite chicken Caesar salad with a friend who has been deeply involved in workplace issues, and this was the heart of our conversation. I began with: "Tell me what is going on with your clients these days? I have never seen such job anxiety and worry about the future."

We were chewing on both salad and the subject of what is really happening with today's workforce. As a professional coach and speaker, I listen to thousands of corporate participants who live in the trenches. I hear what they say about their lives at work.

I continued my workplace observations: "My coaching clients seem reluctant to jump or even get seen on the radar. One said 'The headcounters are everywhere looking to cut more heads, but unless they move a doublewide bunkhouse onto the parking lot, I don't think I can be here any more hours.'"

Career glue™ at work - that stops us in dead in our chairs

As an executive coach, I see qualified employees who are reluctant to jump jobs or even apply for promotions they deserve. What I hear and sense is their underlying feeling of uncertainty about their work lives today and what might happen to them tomorrow. Their views of the risks seem to overpower their natural desire to grow and spread their wings. Even the high-tech folks with specific skill sets seem rooted in place. And the result of this turmoil is we sit rooted at our desks not knowing what step to take next.

What is the cause of this career glue? It seems to be generated by future fear, or yesterday's job crisis or just living in a shaky work atmosphere in which you fear the foundation is collapsing under you.

We live in a society increasingly defined by its insecurities. We get pounded daily with fear-based marketing and broadcast news, sometimes fabricated out of the thinnest news stories. We fear the loss of our jobs, our health, our money, our relationships, our sense of control.

Reframing America

We are experiencing big changes in the way business works in America. Our society is reframing its thinking about the role of work, jobs and security. Generations of our families have placed job security on a pedestal. We have a strong cultural message that the consequence of losing the "job" is in effect to risk ruining your life.

Thus job loss is a fear that is deeply embedded in many aspects of our day-to-day lives, yet we live in a country that swears by our love of freedom. My Australian colleague tells of his puzzlement coming to America and seeing all the advertisements that feature freedom as a selling point. Freedom trucks, freedom to drive wherever you want and whenever you want are all highly prized parts of our culture. Our Fourth of July freedom parades and fireworks are as American as apple pie.

He then pondered why Americans, who so cherish freedom, surrender their freedom every day when they get to the employee entrance where they work.

If you watch the movie *The Full Monty*, beneath the story line of unemployed steel workers struggling to make money, there is a more powerful story line of what happens if you don't have a job in this culture.

One character is even driven to attempt suicide.

Fear drives the movie plot to the point where the actors put on a male strip act to make money and restore their standing in the community. **No Job = No Worth!**

A generational timeline for the past several decades shows that our country and our world have reeled from wars, possibility of wars, saber rattling and catastrophic events such as September 11. Where is safety? Someone wrote that September 10, 2001 was the last day we lived with a sense of safety. A hiccup in the Middle East sends traders to radically rethink their options on the oil market. We deal daily with an apparently unending supply of fearful situations.

Fear surrounds us and stops our own productivity

Fear drives us, and it is not only fear of economic havoc, nuclear weapons and war but other terrors that are in our subconscious.

Downsizing, productivity increases, workforce reduction, relationship status, health needs, kids college costs, keeping our Bloomberg rating high, even greed can be the father of this fear phenomenon. If the Big Three automakers can't guarantee any job security, who can?

We need to find and get rid of whatever is keeping us from jumping off the high diving board into living the life we want to lead. Fear of taking the leap also keeps us from becoming the best at what we were built to do for ourselves and our organizations.

> *Whatever you fear most has no power... it is your fear that has the power.*
>
> - **Oprah Winfrey**

To live our lives successfully, we must know who and what we really are. That discovery takes willingness to move beyond our fear, incorporate our desire and intention and move into action. But if we are not willing to move beyond the fear, our risk is to live a life half lived. Or live someone else's idea of what our life should be.

Even though we may do it perfectly, it will never be as satisfying, easy and effective as living our own life. This book is about overcoming that fear that holds us back from knowing, and expressing, who and what we really are.

I don't want to walk on fire
– I just want a better job

At the beginning of this journey, as we munched through our Caesar salads and discussed workplace concerns, our core focus was on untangling the emotional processes that keep us locked in place. Where we, often unknowingly, permit our future to be totally in the hands of others. Are we judged constantly on a shifting scale in which we never quite know where we stand?

We talked about finding the solution to this way of thinking. What tools can help us dig our way out?

When I looked in the bookstores, most business books and even the so-called "self-help" business titles didn't help me with the needs and challenges of getting where I needed to go. Even the quick fixes in the motivational seminars seem to offer no solution that lasts longer than the drive home. I don't want to walk on fire – I just want a better job, a feeling of security and a sense that I matter.

Seminars gone astray and why I wrote this book

A good example of what I mean about few resources to help us get unstuck was an article in *Fast Company* magazine. Its article on workplace emotion (i.e. fear) featured an interview with an employee who talked about how good intentions from her boss on reassuring everyone went terribly astray. In fact, it left them only with fear.

She related how her boss had attended a Tom Peters motivational seminar and had come back all fired up. But the supervisor took the quotes from Peters' seminar out of context and created his own PowerPoint staff presentation. One slide read:

We're all going to be replaced by workers in India.

We're all going to die by our own hands or at the hands of our competition.

Clearly, not so motivational. Leaders lead.

With no ready fix on the book shelves or at the podium, I began to seek a solution not already on the shelf. I saw that I needed to fill in the blanks in this subject.

What do you fear?

In starting my own speaking business after years of management at Saks Fifth Avenue and Neiman Marcus, I quickly learned the self employment fears around getting health care, handling cash flow and more.

Today, my clients often uncover their own business dreams during coaching sessions, dreams such as owning their own restaurant, tech firm or specialty retail store.

I get concerned watching these same clients club their dreams to death because of their fear of not being up to the task of handling basic business operational issues such as paperwork, accounting and losing their company healthcare benefits.

What do we fear? Where is fear stored in our brains? Do we throw out other parts of our brain to make room for the fear section?

Fear makes us stupid

When we work in a fear-based environment, we in fact train our brains to live fearfully. Because the brain changes in response to how we use it, the more time we spend in an anxious state, the more developed these lower regions become. Worse, when we are not exercising the higher brain regions, which is the source of all our artistic/scientific/creative endeavors and the connections that modulate the fear circuits, these too are weakened comparatively.

So fear stops us, literally, dead in our tracks. Fear literally can make us stupid. Brain researchers have found that fear is mediated by the most ancient parts of the brain. These regions take control when we are frightened and basically turn off the areas responsible for rational thought.

The amygdala, known as the fear center, one of the most primitive brain regions, overrides the prefrontal cortex, which handles working memory and executive function. "When those deep brain areas are active, they shanghai your cortical neurons," says psychiatrist Edward Hallowell, author of *CrazyBusy*. "Your IQ plummets. Your creativity, your sense of humor — all of that disappears. You're stupid."

This is not just a metaphor: quite literally, these primitive regions control our actions and prevent abstract thoughts from occurring to us when we are terrified. The pattern can be seen on brain scans.

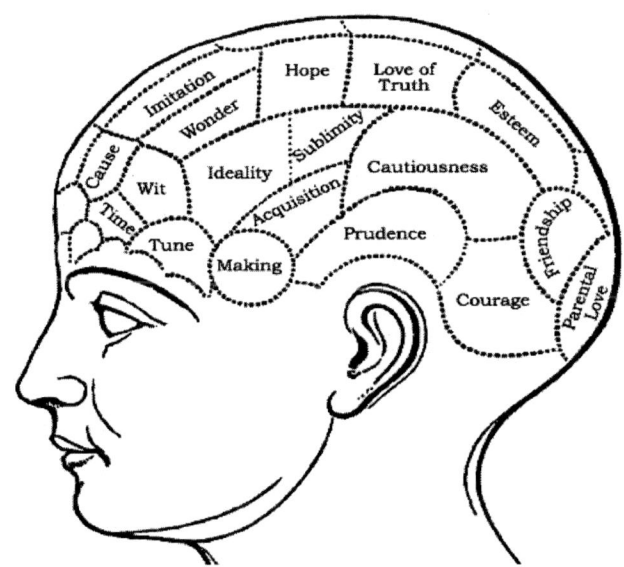

*Life offers you a thousand chances ...
all you have to do is take one.*

- Under the Tuscan Sun, movie poster tag line

Life's too short to wear tight clothes

We avoid what we fear. Avoiding what we fear only strengthens the fear and makes us less prepared to deal with it in the future.

As I named this fear, my speeches moved into challenging themes such as *Life's Too Short To Wear Tight Clothes* and *Stop Sitting On Your Bar Code.* These topics were about creating change and increasing your personal branding to get unstuck.

To support the message, I gathered current data on workplace stress and its causes. As I reframed my thinking, even my existing programs such as time management had new perspectives. In my *Targeting Time* workshops at Southern Methodist University, I began my speech with "wasting time by doing something you enjoy is probably not wasting time."

Hey look at me. I matter.

After that pivotal and insightful initial lunch, I went back to my office and began the process of connecting the dots I was seeing with the current job and career environment.

Since much of our anxiety concerns the fear of losing our jobs, I wanted to find out exactly why we lose jobs. The Harvard University Bureau of Vocational Guidance studied thousands of men and women who had been fired. Their data revealed that for every one person who lost a job for failure to do their work, two people lost their jobs for their inability to deal with other people successfully.

People who make themselves matter develop significant people skills. Building on that, the Carnegie Institute of Technology concluded that only fifteen percent of job success is due to skill set training, intellect and job skills. However, eighty-five percent of job success is due to personality factors. So, to make yourself matter, you must be able to work successfully with other people.

The purpose of this book, my speech and my work is NOT to find out what is wrong with people but how we can build on their right qualities. **Martin Seligman**, author of *Authentic Happiness*, found that the "highest success in living and deepest emotional satisfaction comes from building and using your signature strengths."

Now I was able to put a name to the strengths and human qualities necessary to banish indecision and doubt from our work life thinking, get into action and become the productive person you were built to be.

What Dale Carnegie discovered

It has been reported that **Dale Carnegie**, the American writer and lecturer and developer of famous courses in self-improvement, salesmanship, corporate training and public speaking, in looking back on his life saw that worry and fear were the two forces that held him back from achieving his dreams. It was because of this awareness that he came to develop the famous Dale Carnegie Course as a practical means for overcoming this worry and fear.

I now had a name to describe the **"Simple Truths"** that can promote and reward the insights learned from climbing out of negative thinking and into a life that is happy, joyous, productive and less stressful.

I was developing a new way of living that says, "Hey look at me. I matter!"

I knew that these **"10 Simple Truths,"** if used, would release us from the tyranny of stress, job dissatisfaction and fear of the future.

If we begin to include one, two or more of these ten initiatives in our lives, not only will it change our thinking but our behavior as well, since our thinking influences our attitude which determines much of our behavior.

What is the key to matter?

The key to confronting and beating fear is to **Make Yourself Matter** today. By doing well what we love to do, we make ourselves valuable to our communities and to our organizations and stop wasting time working on weaknesses. This book is NOT your annual "self-review."

Make Yourself Matter folks are the type of people that *"get it."* They know what needs to be done, and they know how to do it and get the support to turn talent into performance.

They love their work, they're passionate about the results they produce and everyone around them catches the fever.

What we find is these people are indispensable. Literally, they keep the organization running. From Admins to CEOs, they matter by what and how they do their jobs.

To put it another way, they are *"value added"* resources. When cutbacks occur, any staff trimmers would think many times before letting them go because they make things work. And if they do get cut, other organizations are quick to pick them up because their skills and confidence are readily apparent.

The difference between being famous and being recognized

The branding of ourselves as indispensable is not about becoming famous. It is about becoming known and recognized. There is a huge difference between these two points on the fame continuum.

Becoming well known, or at least well known among your prospective customers or internal connections, is the single most valuable element in the entire connection process.

Some of us struggle with the idea of becoming well known. In my *Maximizing U* workshop on personal branding, we define how to get recognized within our organization. Becoming well known has many business benefits including building on resources from others. Plus, the networking opportunities are plentiful when you are known to others. Consider these two, now famous, people.

Tiger Woods doesn't make sales calls. People call him. Oprah Winfrey doesn't make sales calls. People call her.

Believe it or not, these two people did not start out famous. They both built their skills until they were recognized by those around them. Ergo, now they are two famous people.

The more recognized you are, the more people will *want* to connect with you. When you are an unknown, you have to reach out to make the connection.

Obviously you can't go from being a relative nobody to being recognized overnight. The key is to start with small actions.

Strategy

What actions will help you *Make Yourself Matter* and emphasize your signature strengths. One big first step is to have a plan.

I travel a great deal and I use a road map to get me where I need to go. There are many strategy questions, but here are some of the most common.

- What are you trying to do?
- Who do you need to get it done?
- What is the obstacle you face?
- What assets and resources do you have?
- How much do you know?
- How will you know its working?

I found I needed a strategy to develop my research on this topic. I wanted to find out what others had in their heads regarding corporate fear.

To begin, I used the Internet and email to send my questionnaire out on how to *Make Yourself Matter*. I began my worldwide research of these truths by asking:

- How do you make yourself matter, and what does it mean to you?
- What are the unique abilities in the work place that enable you to *Make Yourself Matter*?
- What are the signature strengths that stand both the test of time and career transitions?
- What gives us both hope and direction that what we do has lasting value?

As the responses flooded in, they quickly divided into categories that eventually fit into what I now call the "10 simple truths." They are the core of the book and they are key to engagement in the life of the business.

I am constantly asked, are there just 10? There are many, and each time I speak, people come to me and share their own powerful stories of how these 10 truths relate to their lives. Their conversations give me more data and topics to the truths. The list goes on.

Your goals are the road maps that guide you and show you what is possible for your life.
- Lew Brown

Make Yourself Matter is a thin slice of reel life

I often cringe when I remember the movie *About Schmidt*, with Jack Nicholson. He won the 2003 Golden Globe award for best actor in this drama which opens with a terrible scene: he sits in his suit watching the wall clock tick slowly to 5:00 p.m. on his last day on the job. The only sound is the clock ticking. No one comes in. The office is stripped of any sign of his 40 years on the job and his files containing the results of his work are neatly stacked in the corner.

The next movie scene is the typical rubber-chicken retirement party where coworkers sum up the career of the retiree.

Jack's replacement, an aggressive young man, stands up to say a few words about him. It's like a living eulogy, only everyone is eating chicken instead of clutching a handkerchief in a funeral home. All the guy can say about Jack is the most hallow cliché that Nicholson has left "big shoes" for him to fill.

Big Shoes!! What does that say about someone? Meanwhile, the whole room senses the new boss is having to struggle even to say that much. And then, two weeks later when Jack comes back to have lunch with his replacement, he sees all his files sitting on the loading dock ready to be thrown into the dumpster. Big shoes indeed.

The point is that Nicholson's colleagues have almost nothing to say about him after he has served 40 years at an insurance company. The scene is awful only because it's so real. Every day tens of thousands of people retire, and their coworkers find it hard to make the most cursory remarks about them.

People who make themselves matter never worry about this scene because they are too busy to think about it and all around them are co-workers and customers who constantly turn to them and who would mourn their absence, even for a week's vacation, with great regret.

Today, few of us work in any one company for that length of time. This makes the need to make ourselves matter of more urgency. With a shorter time line, we need to communicate our strengths to our associates and customers more quickly using communication tools that carry the message clearly and timely.

> *The more value you bring, the higher you will go. Create value that is greater than price, quality and service. If two products of similar price and service are offered, the sales professional with greater perceived value will win.*
>
> - Tim Wackel, sales training guru

This is the story of *Make Yourself Matter*, an idea born over a Caesar Salad lunch with friends that became a critical conversation and grew to bigger discussions and is now a book. It is the story of how input from friends and strangers, both here and all over the world, have been incorporated and enriched these concepts.

To be honest, the list is never complete. Each time it is shared, new ideas and insights get incorporated. Now participants send me emails with stories about making themselves matter. They share how this process adds value to themselves and how it put a handle on something inside them.

Life is calling. How will you answer?

Make Yourself Matter is the bottom-line for all working people to reach the level of success they want. When working for someone else, or on your own, one has to "really matter" to be valued and deeply appreciated. We all want to be around people that matter.

If you want to go against the way things have always gone in your life, think about how your plan to make yourself matter is constructed. It doesn't matter if you're at a high-tech company, an admin at the City, or even a stay at home person. The key is to start the action. Enrolling for your associate's degree counts as much as an MBA in the eyes of a hiring person who measures action more than intent.

Often the difference between a successful man and a failure is not one's better abilities or ideas, but the courage that one has to bet on his ideas, to take a calculated risk, and to act.

- Maxwell Maltz

Passion is one of the hidden secrets to making yourself matter. We are drawn to passion even if we disagree with the point of it all. In this environment you want to be passionate about what you are doing and what you represent.

When you matter so does your business. Your clients will recognize the enthusiasm and passion and respond to you. Once again, we all want to be around people that "get it," that matter, that know how to get things done.

In every business, efficient, capable, responsible, commitment oriented people are important. Those who *really matter* and get recognized accordingly are unstoppable!

Choose to live a life that matters.

#10
Pull off at least one miracle for a client.

Clients don't want to hear about the labor pains. They just want to see the baby.

—Andy Lansing, CEO, Levy Restaurants

"If you've got an emergency, we can work a miracle," said Steve Driediger, owner of Miracle Print in Alberta, Canada, during an interview in *Fast Company*.

Do you believe in miracles at work like Steve?

Perhaps we need to chat a bit more about what makes up a miracle in business. In the business of sports, we hear lots about miracles.

Beliefnet.com tells the story of a gripping sports miracle. At the height of the Cold War, some American college kids, really a handful of amateurs, and a second-tier coach won the gold medal in the 1980 Lake Placid

Olympics. They defeated a Soviet team long believed to be the greatest hockey power in Olympic history.

Seeing is believing

We all watched the game footage and we've thrilled with the Disney movie. We've heard the famous call of the game's final seconds: "Do you believe in miracles?" Still, this miraculous moment amazes like few others.

In fact, the culture of sports is almost entirely made up of miraculous moments that become the legend of the game and a shared experience never to be forgotten.

Can't we have work-related business miracles as well, such as getting something done for a client that blows them away? You see the need, and you do it. Yet, you do not trumpet your work all over the company.

I love to tell legendary service stories. At Neiman Marcus, **Stanley Marcus** helped create many of them. Once a customer asked for a dress in a certain shade of buff yellow she had seen in a painting. Mr. Marcus went to New York, had a fabric dyed to order and made up a dress especially for her for only $42.00 dollars. Which was more the miracle: Mr. Stanley's customer concern or a $42.00 Neiman Marcus price tag?

The next season, Neiman's "buff yellow" was a bestseller and a fashion hit. It was a win-win for all. As Mr. Stanley repeated to us often, "if it's not good for the customer, it's not good for Neiman Marcus."

Consumers are statistics. Customers are people.
— **Stanley Marcus**

An excellent example of pulling off a miracle for a client concerns a manager for a property management company. Her homeowner-association clients had misplaced their club house storage key and couldn't get their supplies out for their annual HOA Saturday-night block party. They called the management company hotline for help and she heard their call.

This miracle worker left her own dinner party on a Saturday night to drive to her office and locate an extra key for the HOA storage building and deliver it to them.

Her story demonstrates the key point of Simple Truth # 10 in that the company owner never heard about it till the HOA president called her to rave about the employee.

Steve Driediger, the Canadian *Miracle Print* president, doesn't have to take out newspaper ads telling about his good work in pulling off miracles in his printing niche. His customers do it for him.

Was it a miracle for Miracle Print to get a difficult job done well? Well, it was probably the usual blood, sweat and tears that miracles often take. The challenge of miracles is that they appear ordinary because of the skill in which they are implemented.

Show and Tell

John Royer is a human resource industry executive who shared the following story of his own about someone pulling off a miracle. You be the judge.

When the phone rang, it was my senior vice president calling me on short notice asking me to bring the presentation I had recently developed to the meeting room so he could show some other executives. After assuring him we could do it in 30 minutes, I panicked as I put the phone down.

'Janice, can you help me find a projector while I review the presentation a last time?' Janice, my administrative assistant, contacted Facilities, but all their AV (audio/visual) equipment was being used by other people. Next she called two other administrative assistants to see if they knew where she could get one. Again, no luck. Her third attempt to contact someone was more fruitful as she was given two names of people to call who 'might' be able to help her.

Within minutes of the presentation, the administrative assistant was hustling to another floor to get the projector she had found. She met me at the conference room as my guests sat down, and she was as calm and collected as if the projector had been at her desk the entire time.

The presentation was saved due to her resourcefulness. Someone else in that position might have just come into my office and told me they were unable to find a projector. She made herself valuable to me by using her initiative, resourcefulness and dedication to help me. I knew I could always count on her to find a way to get things done.

What was the benefit to Janice in making herself *valuable*? "I remembered her every time it was merit, bonus or stock nomination time," says John Royer.

Hail Mary

You face a difficult challenge at work. You work like the devil to make it happen and--you do. Quietly. Maybe it's not a miracle the Pope might recognize, but for you it feels really good. The customer is thrilled, and you have a good feeling about taking care of the problem.

However some may feel that a "miracle" is the opposite of your style of work. If you believe you provide consistent quality in all of your work you avoid by nature any *"showboating"* that miracle might imply. Relax. This is not what Simple Truth #10 is about.

What's a "Hail Mary" football pass as made famous by **Roger Staubach**? As aptly defined, a *Hail Mary pass* is a forward pass made in desperation, with only a very small chance of success. The typical Hail Mary is a very long forward pass thrown at or near the end of a half where there is no realistic possibility for any other play to work, though the most famous were thrown at the end of a game.

The phrase derives from the Catholic prayer to the Virgin Mary. The point is that the success of such a pass is so unlikely that it would need divine intervention to work, such as a miracle. Well, I don't think that pulling off the miracle of Simple Truth # 10 is like that.

Customer service is king

I learned so much from Mr. Stanley in my years at Neiman Marcus. I always say that I got my Ph. D. at NM in good taste and good service, plus the opportunity to see how a successful organization comes together. Consider these insights from Stanley Marcus who continued to be actively speaking and consulting till his 90's.

> ". . . . In a free economy, in which customers are free to exercise a choice in their purchases, superior service provides the competitive advantage that is needed when qualities are comparable."

> "It is impossible," Marcus wrote, "to create a service-oriented business unless the boss learns to think like a customer."

> "Once he does," Marcus continued, "everything has a tendency to fall into place, and customers rush to join the chorus of praise for a farsighted management."

> "Little things often give us the signs of good management. For example, taxi cab companies that have good dispatchers and who make an effort to understand the caller, stores that carry your packages to your car. . . ."

> "These are not tricks, but are devices that prove the management's determination not only to think like a customer, but to act like one also. The most important indicator is that they care about you. All of us appreciate care."

People who make themselves matter work to get the job done. They create miracles over long gestation periods. The miracles they create can be tangible and more often, in the case of people development, intangible. Shouldn't all of my work be a miracle for my client? Author **Og Mandino** - in his book, *The Greatest Miracle in the World* is asked to define a miracle. "It's something that happens contrary to the laws of nature or science...a temporary suspension of one of these laws."

Author **David d'Alessandro** turns the miracle story one twist further when he suggests, "Why not teach others that they can perform a miracle with their lives?"

Don't quit five minutes before the miracle.

Carl's Final Word

Many of us already do good work for our customers. The key is keeping our mouths shut afterwards.

Pull off at least one miracle for a client.

Put your knowledge to work.

Practical Applications.

#9
Be an authority.

It's so beautifully arranged on the plate -- you know someone's fingers have been all over it.

- Julia Child on nouvelle cuisine

Knowing what we do well

I remember that Julia was in her element. Sitting on the floor with her back against the wall, and filtered sunlight pouring in, she began to talk. This section of *Make Yourself Matter* is dedicated to Julia Child who discovered what she loved to do, built her life and her reputation on doing it and showed us the way to be an authority.

In executive coaching, I frequently probe new clients to find out what they feel they do well. In fact, I ask each of them to define the area of work they really love to do.

Why is this hard to do?

If I asked them what they don't do well, the list would probably flow quickly. This remains a puzzler about human nature and/or our culture of minimizing our assets.

When we define what we love to do and do well, we can leverage our business expertise in that area.

Knowledge is the antidote to fear.

- Ralph Waldo Emerson

Becoming an authority can be seen clearly in the life and work of **Julia Child**. When I was Director of Epicure at Neiman Marcus, Julia and her husband Paul came to

Dallas for the French Fortnight celebration which was a signature event at Neiman Marcus. Julia had just produced her series of cooking videos on preparing French cuisine at home.

I was 32 when I started cooking; up until then, I just ate.

- Julia Child

When she finished her video signings with hundreds of customers, I suggested we enjoy lunch at the Zodiac, the famous NM restaurant. But Julia had other ideas. At her suggestion, I pulled some bread, meat and cheeses from the French Deli in the store, plus *several* bottles of wine, and the three of us settled onto the floor of a large fitting room off the sales floor with big windows flooding the room with October sunshine.

Julia was in her element. Sitting on the floor with her back against the wall, with filtered sunlight pouring in, she began to talk. During the course of several bottles of wine, Julia and Paul told me their stories of their World War II wartime work with the forerunner to today's Central Intelligence Agency. After the war, they moved to France where Julia explored her new interest in French cooking. After cooking school and cookbook collaboration, she gradually developed into a respected authority on the nuances of French cuisine.

Non-cooks think it's silly to invest two hours' work in two minutes' enjoyment; but if cooking is evanescent, so is the ballet.

- Julia Child

Upon returning to Boston, Julia and PBS discovered each other, and the rest became television and cuisine history. In the process, Julia Child became an authority on a style of cooking that had seemed unapproachable to many American recreational cooks.

When I suggest that clients become **an authority** on what they do, Julia represents an excellent example we can all follow. She was a tall, gangly American who translated French cooking into something we could all do, and she did it with humor. With her fluty voice and towering build, adorned with pearls and her Smith College hairdo, she captivated her audience when she said, "Hello."

In 1962, WGBH television viewers enjoyed her demonstration of how to cook an omelet so much that when *The French Chef* debuted February 11, 1963, it was immediately successful. When asked why she was always slathering butter on chickens, her sly response was *"the chickens really liked it."*

You don't have to cook fancy or complicated masterpieces -- just good food from fresh ingredients.

- Julia Child

13

Julia found what she loved to do. What do you love to do? **What have people told you that you do well?** Who would pay you to do what you love to do and do well?

Many people who become authorities are self made and self taught, even when they have already achieved some level of success in what they do. Their hunger for learning propels them into the next areas of their life challenges.

From the kitchen to the garage

A good example of that hunger for growth is **Carl Sewell**, an auto dealer who is well known throughout Texas and beyond. Carl is not the typical TV infomercial huckster wearing a clown suit, standing by cars propped with balloons and sale stickers. Instead, he both wrote and rewrote the book on successfully running an auto business.

Ask customers what they want and give it to them again and again.

- Carl Sewell

At 28, Carl had taken over his family's Dallas Cadillac business in which he had labored for 14 years. He maintained the good family business name but had no clear path on where to take it. What he needed to achieve the dream in his head went beyond his own knowledge base.

He needed expertise and he hired it. With a consultant who took a close look at how the business was currently running, he made decisions on what kind of people and operations were needed to go forward. They were the toughest of decisions, but without the right team, the game would never be won.

The process Carl went through to transform his business from uninspired to much-copied is a remarkable story that he told in his recently reissued best seller, *Customers For Life*.

With more than 600,000 copies sold, the book tells how he reinvented his company's culture so that extraordinary customer service became its watchword. In fact, the radio advertisements for the Sewell Family of dealerships all have one thing in common--they only talk about service. Yep, that's it--service. No daily specials or tune up messages. The commercials are always about upscale service in both humorous and informational ways. And they ring true because everyone in the trade area knows they are true.

Being nice to people is just 20% of providing good customer service. The important part is designing systems that allow you to do the job right the first time. All the smiles in the world aren't going to help if your product or service is not what the customer wants.

- Carl Sewell

Carl left his competition in his rearview mirror with nothing to talk about in their ads without appearing crass. More importantly, to keep the sales side supported, he reframed the typical dreaded showroom encounter into a dialogue that has less to do with the notion of always having to compete on price and more about getting what you want in a car.

His publisher, Random House, posted on its website this detail on the phenomenon that is Carl Sewell:

> Carl revealed the secret of getting customers to return again and again in *Customers for Life* which draws on his incredible success in transforming his Dallas Cadillac dealership into the second largest in America. Sewell focuses on the expectations and demands of contemporary consumers and employees, showing that businesses can remain committed to quality service in the fast-paced new millennium by sticking to his time-proven approach--*figure out what customers want and make sure they get it*.

Carl Sewell developed what he called the Ten Commandments that provide the essential service guidelines, including these:

> • **Under promise, over deliver**: Never disappoint your customers by charging them more than they planned. Always beat your estimate or throw in an extra service free of charge.
>
> • **No complaints? Something's wrong**: If you never ask your customers what else they want, how are you going to give it to them?
>
> • **Measure everything**: Telling your employees to

do their best won't work if you don't know how they can improve.

• **Borrow, borrow, borrow**: Sewell, for example, learned about hospitality from Japanese culture, cleanliness from Disney, and politeness from his mother.

Too many people overvalue what they are not and undervalue what they are.

- Malcolm Forbes

By becoming an authority, like Julia Child or Carl Sewell, we own the "expert" label for what we do. When your business depends on you, you have job security or excellent new job options. Being an authority on you and what you do well is the best guarantee for employment happiness in a world that sometimes forgets how work flies by when we are doing what we love.

Be an authority – on you!

Carl's Final Word

Authorities come in all shapes and sizes, from my Vietnamese cleaners who can get marinara sauce from my jacket to my "nerd" friends who can fix my vast office electronic empire. They love to do what they do well. Julia Child loved cooking and became America's authority on cooking and French cuisine. Stanley Marcus loved fur retailing, and it is estimated he personally sold more than $10 million worth of furs to Neiman Marcus customers.

Be An Authority.

Put your knowledge to work.

Be An Authority.

#8

Understand and lead others on the concept of innovation.

Innovation and how to achieve it is still king of the hill in business thought fashions. With all that thinking, why are companies still not innovating the way they want to?

- Dr. E. Ted Prince

I love to tell the story of Deborah Adler who was working on a design project for her master's degree when she found out that her grandmother had accidentally taken her grandfather's medicine.

She saw that her grandmother's RX bottles were practically identical. From identifying that need, she believed she could design a better system for prescription bottles. That prescription mix-up was the design genesis of one of the biggest changes in medicine packaging since childproof lids.

Target Store pharmacies now have embraced her new line of containers with the little red upside-down bottles that fit right in with their Michael Graves cheap, but, good design philosophy.

But the packaging is more than a pretty face. This packaging is such a buzz topic that Target now features the bottles in its print ads. I got a prescription filled at Target just to see the difference in bottles.

Target's prescription bottles are *"way cool"* and so much easier to handle and read. Is this a waste of innovation talent? Think of how many prescriptions get filled every day and who uses them.

Innovations in the Medicine Cabinet

- **A different colored band** on each bottle for each member of the family just like with electric toothbrushes.

- **A flat surface** that displays drug and dosage information on the front and warnings on the back. No more wrap-around vision problems which one has when reading the old-style containers.

- **A special pocket** for the patient drug advisory sheet that fits inside the label.

Innovation can be in any part of any business, and telling the story can be half the fun. Innovation can be tasty as this next story will reveal.

Innovation you can taste

You sit down to eat in one of the oldest restaurants in New York City. The atmosphere is delightful with crisp white linens, the bustle of busy waiters and the hum of happy diners.

Soon your meal arrives followed by the bill. Your hamburger was $41.00.

Can you imagine a $41.00 Kobe beef hamburger? That burger was introduced by the venerable *Old Homestead Steak House* on the west side of Manhattan near the old meat market area.

Who would be silly enough to pay $41.00 for a hamburger? Apparently there were enough silly folks who would, because on the first day, they sold over 200 of them, including some to major entertainment figures.

They got great buzz with $41.00 burgers on their grill. The steak house got great business and even greater publicity for their business through a single act of innovation.

Confusing creativity and innovation

One of the biggest leadership mistakes we make is confusing creativity and innovation. Innovation refers to changes to products, processes or services. The often unspoken goal of innovation is to solve a problem.

On the other hand, creativity has a very different approach. **George Keller**, an American architect and engineer, said, "Creativity consists largely of re-arranging what we know in order to find out what we do not know." When we know what we do not know, we have actually made huge strides in thinking. Filling in our own blanks is the challenge we most often face.

Those who dream by day are cognizant of many things which escape those who dream only by night.

- Edgar Allen Poe

Although creativity is popularly associated with art and literature, it is also an essential part of business innovation and invention.

With my luxury retail background, I was always grateful that both Saks Fifth Avenue and Neiman Marcus were brimming with highly creative people who not only created product, but they were also superb on the storytelling side in creating advertising to help sell it.

If you want things to stay as they are, things will have to change.

- Giuseppe de Lampedusa,
  Sicilian Novelist on Innovation

The famous Fortnight in-store celebrations from Neiman Marcus were an example of innovation that was helped along with huge doses of creativity. The challenge was to create a center of business between back-to-school and Christmas business periods. Ergo, the October Fortnights became that center of interest, and for generations of Texans it was their first real peak into exotic foreign countries.

Each year, the creative challenge was to take a newly chosen country or region and salute it through merchandise, through cuisine and most importantly, through the creative people of the country. While an expense, the Fortnight celebrations created significant customer interest over the years and embedded Neiman Marcus into the culture and the entire city.

If you take care of the customers, they come back. If you take care of the products, they don't come back.

- Stanley Marcus

Because of the illusive nature of creativity, entire industries have now developed to create categories such as business names, products, revamping of old products and more. The work of innovation is not so illusory.

Creativity is a topic of such importance in the workplace that there has been much research, and many consultants have put their own spin on it. I developed my own "team role" shorthand descriptors based on the countless hours of coaching and workshop work I have conducted.

Creating high-performance, innovative, workplace teams by understanding, and using behavioral preferences

- **The generator** is the new-idea-every day person. New mousetraps are a specialty of the generator, and in fact, the natural outlet of their thinking. They are great to get the ball rolling with either taking something old and reframing it into something new--and more appealing--creating a new approach to often old problems. If unchecked or untapped for their creative vein, the creator may well become either Über creative or withdrawn. Their motto is *"Goody, let's figure out how to get some new ideas on this."*

- Next on the scale is **the early adopter**. The favorite role of early adopters on a work team is to take an early stage idea and make it better. They bring enthusiasm and skill to the ideas created by the generator. Their motto is *"Let me help get it going."*

- One of the least appreciated roles in any team environment is that of **the challenger**. These folks are often accused of throwing buckets of icy cold water on new thinking and ideas. Their preferred activity is reviewing plans and looking for loose ends and possible flaws that their predecessors could well have left undone on the innovation team grid. Their motto is *"There is a lot of unfinished work in this."*

- **The implementer** is the last in line, and implementers want to take the ball and run with it. With their orderly thinking, they like a plan and they like to work that plan. Outcomes are better when they are on the job with their quality orientation and attention to details. Their motto is *"Let's get this show on the road."*

  - Carl Youngberg, on creating leadership in workplace innovation

Learning the art of using different styles to make yourself and your team matter

In addition to working on team preferences, I use these four categories of workplace behavioral roles because I need to be able to say quickly to a client what team role that I see in operation. I find that successful team members don't do the same thing at the same time. They each do the right thing at the right time.

Knowing **HOW** we work is critical in *Make Yourself Matter*. In fact, by knowing our preferred roles in innovation and teamwork, we edge our way to the top of the indispensable list. Test drive your favorite style from the previous page.

Which one of these innovation team roles is your greatest talent? One of the key ways to make yourself matter is to see if your current job fits your talent.

Are you expected to be a creative generator when in your heart you are an adopter? A major failing in management responsibilities is assuming that managers and staff who are given the responsibility to innovate will actually do so.

The expectation that sticky or tricky situations will be fixed with creative and satisfying solutions can lead to management disappointment when the solution is not forthcoming.

A better expectation for management is discovering their work team strengths in the first place.

You are reading this book for a reason. I suspect that you are ready for some innovation in your life.

Every team member can contribute for an engaged team

In working with teams on how to become innovative, collaborative, and integrated, I often give the teams a small light bulb.

As we begin the project for the teams, much of the awareness about how people perform in teams is often the same size as the light bulb they have been given.

As we continue, and the ah-ha moments begin to occur in which the team colleagues become collaborators, I give out higher wattage light bulbs.

This continues throughout the training.

When we are finished, I give the leaders three-way bulbs to remind them they can vary the wattage and determine how much energy is needed to invest in each of their projects.

- Carl Youngberg

Think outside the suggestion box

At Toyota, the company requested that each employee submit two suggestions each month for improvements. Not only does the company request them, it listens to them. Associates made more than three million suggestions in one year. And the company acted on 80 percent of them.

But the real crowning glory is that Toyota set up a system to nurture suggestions and evaluate and implement the majority of those suggestions. The message from Toyota is that they listen – and they respond.

Just think what the impact of millions of improvement suggestions would have on a firm.

Being comfortable in our business is very, very dangerous.

- Daniel Lamarre, President and COO, Cirque du Soleil

 **Carl's Final Word**

The business landscape is littered with the wrecks and relics of failed companies. Their failures often happen due to a lack of innovation. Make Yourself Matter is about creativity and practicing innovation.

Understand and lead others in the concept and importance of innovation.

Put your knowledge to work.

The Path to Simple Truth # 8

Practical applications.

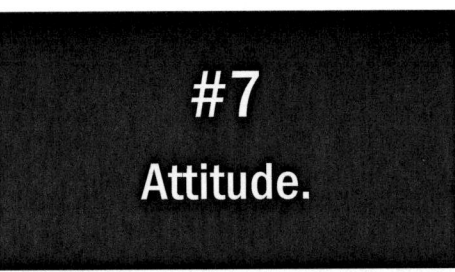

#7
Attitude.

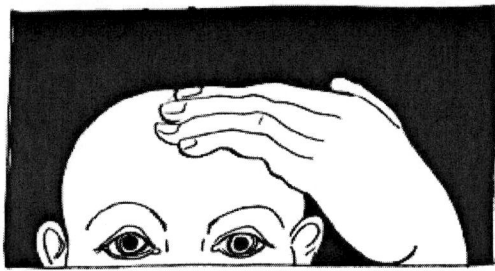

There once was a woman who woke up one morning, looked in the mirror and noticed she had only three hairs on her head.

"Well," she said, "I think I'll braid my hair today." So she did and she had a wonderful day.

The next day she woke up, looked in the mirror and saw that she had only two hairs on her head.

"H-M-M," she said, "I think I'll part my hair down the middle today." So she did and she had a grand day.

The next day she woke up, looked in the mirror and noticed that she had only one hair on her head.

"Well," she said, "Today I'm going to wear my hair in a pony tail." So she did and she had a fun, fun day.

The next day she woke up, looked in the mirror and noticed that there wasn't a single hair on her head.

"YEAH!" she exclaimed, "I don't have to fix my hair today!"

   - Anonymous

Attitude is everything

Some of my best bosses were stealth bosses who led by pushing me along even when I didn't quite realize what was going on. A favorite was **Delora Bewley**, my first boss in Kansas City when I worked days at a city jail and went to graduate school in psychology at night.

Delora was a diminutive woman of color who had a graduate degree in social work, and she dreamed of stopping young inner-city men and women from returning endlessly to jail and eventually to prison. My job was to set up a prototype social work unit at the jail to intervene in the lives of these young people.

Delora was always a lady and was known for wearing a proper hat even on rough roads or walking the cell blocks.

Make no mistake, she was a velvet hammer who made Margaret Thatcher look like a wuss.

Did everyone welcome us on our mission to help others? Heck no. Some felt that our rehab work was a waste of time and money and resisted. But it was fun to see an ex-Marine argue with Delora. She always won.

What I learned from Delora about attitude was her belief that you could learn a lot from bad bosses just as from good bosses. You just have to be careful what you learn.

I seek constantly to improve my manners and graces, for they are the sugar to which all are attracted.

- Og Mandino

Bad attitudes debilitate
Good attitudes facilitate

The reality of business is that your choice of attitude is one of the most critical business decisions you make each day.   Is my attitude seen as appealing by those around me?

Thoughts always precede behavior. Positive thoughts produce positive results and negative thoughts produce negative results. Yet one study suggested that only five percent of our population knows what kind of thoughts they have.

Packing our attitudes for the car trip

A husband and wife are traveling by car from Key West to Boston. After almost twenty-four hours on the road, they're too tired to continue, and they decide to stop for a rest. They stop at a nice hotel and take a room, but they only plan to sleep for four hours and then get back on the road.

When they checked out four hours later, the desk clerk hands them a bill for $350. The husband explodes and demands to know why the charge is so high.

He tells the clerk although it's a nice hotel, the rooms certainly aren't worth $350.

When the clerk tells him $350 is the standard rate, the man insists on speaking to the manager. The manager appears, listens to the man, and then explains that the hotel has an Olympic-sized pool and a huge conference center that were available for the husband and wife to use.

"But we didn't use them," the man complains.

"Well, they are here, and you could have," explains the manager.

He goes on to explain they could have taken in one of the shows for which the hotel is famous. "The best entertainers from New York, Hollywood and Las Vegas perform here," the manager says.

"But we didn't go to any of those shows," complains the man again.

"Well, we have them, and you could have," the manager replies.

No matter what facility the Manager mentions, the man replies, "But we didn't use it!"

The manager is unmoved, and eventually the man gives up and agrees to pay.

He writes a check and gives it to the manager.

The manager is surprised when he looks at the check. "But sir," he says, this check is only made out for $50."

"That's correct," says the man. "I charged you $300 for sleeping with my wife."

"But I didn't!" exclaims the manager.

"Well, too bad," the man replies. "She was here and you could have."

There are many lessons to be learned from dealing with people.

Stanley Marcus told the story of a man suffering from financial difficulties who was unable to send his daughter off to college and asked about a position at the store for her.

She was hired and when, several years later, she left to be married, Mr. Stanley asked her what was the most important thing she had learned in her time on the sales floor. Her reply was, "people."

She said people could be the meanest and the nicest, and working on the sales floor at Neiman's had given her a chance to learn about both types. She had a learning attitude.

Your attitude is showing

A woman was at her hairdresser's getting her hair styled for a trip to Rome with her husband. She mentioned the trip to the hairdresser, who responded:

"Rome? Why would anyone want to go there? It's crowded and dirty. You're crazy to go to Rome. So, how are you getting there?"

"We're taking Continental," was the reply. "We got a great rate!"

"Continental?" exclaimed the hairdresser." That's a terrible airline. Their planes are old, their flight attendants are ugly and they're always late. So, where are you staying in Rome?"

"We'll be at this exclusive little place over on Rome's Tiber River called Teste."

"Don't go any further. I know that place. Everybody thinks it's gonna be something special and exclusive, but it's really a dump, the worst hotel in the city! The rooms are small, the service is surly and they're overpriced."

"So, whatcha' doing when you get there?"

"We're going to go to see the Vatican and we hope to see the Pope."

"That's rich," laughed the hairdresser. "You and a million other people trying to see him. He'll look the size of an ant. Boy, good luck on this lousy trip of yours. You're going to need it."

A month later, the woman again came in for a hairdo. The hairdresser asked her about her trip to Rome.

"It was wonderful," explained the woman, "not only were we on time in one of Continental's brand new planes, but it was overbooked, and they bumped us up to first class. The food and wine were wonderful, and I had a handsome 28-year-old steward who waited on me hand and foot."

"And the hotel was great! They'd just finished a $5 million dollar remodeling job, and now it's a jewel, the finest hotel in the city. They, too, were overbooked, so they apologized and gave us their owner's suite at no extra charge!"

"Well," muttered the hairdresser, "that's all well and good, but I know you didn't get to see the Pope."

"Actually, we were quite lucky, because as we toured the Vatican, a Swiss Guard tapped me on the shoulder, and explained that the Pope likes to meet some of the visitors, and if I'd be so kind as to step into his private room and wait, the Pope would personally greet me."

"Sure enough, five minutes later, the Pope walked through the door and shook my hand! I knelt down and he spoke a few words to me."

"Oh, really! What'd he say?"

"He said: 'Where'd you get the crappy hairdo?'"

I couldn't fear losing a great job I had never had. I took the opportunity seriously but, at the same time, I had the relaxed confidence of someone who knew he had no real shot.

- Conan O'Brien talking about attitude when auditioning for his late night show

Frankly, I have begun to think that "attitude" is becoming as overused as "self-motivated" in the hiring process. Good people don't "have" an attitude, they *live* an attitude and it shows.

In fact, we all have our attitudes, some are just nicer than others. Good-Attitude people take time to notice others. Their workday commentary is not focused on the traffic jams and crazy driving on the freeways that morning, and they make positive choices on where they put their focus.

> *Wealth follows creativity, it follows street smarts, it follows teamwork, energy, and a don't quit attitude.*
>
> - Jake Steinfeld, fitness guru and author

Changes in Latitudes, Changes in Attitudes is the breakthrough 1977 album by Jimmy Buffett. The album remains the best-selling album of Buffett's career, and it contains his biggest single, *Margaritaville.* While interpreting song lyrics is not my forte, I see a lot of people trying to find better work conditions by frequently changing companies or their latitude.

I refer to this technique as a geographic cure, hoping that another job, boss, company, city, state or country will make for a better place. Yes, 75 percent of us leave our jobs because of bad bosses. But it takes two to tango, and we may well be part of the problem.

Learning to deal with difficult people is one of the greatest lessons we can master and a topic I am often asked about in my program on customer service, *Kiss 'Em On All 4 Cheeks*.

The devil in the corner office

After a lifetime working in high-fashion retailing, I loved the book and movie, *The Devil Wears Prada*. But in fact, the lead character scared me, mostly because I have worked along side too many people just like her. Having worked with people like the crazed magazine editor, I was reminded of the loss of talent by managers who squander their true gifts under ego, or more often, poor self image.

Lauren Weisberger, who wrote *Prada*, describes the book's office environment this way. "A delightfully dishy novel about the all-time most impossible boss in the history of impossible bosses. As things escalate from the merely unacceptable to the downright outrageous, however, Andrea begins to realize that the job a million girls would die for may just kill her. And even if she survives, she has to decide whether or not the job is worth the price of her soul."

I have worked for screamers in my past and I didn't like it then, and I don't like it now. Bullies should be kicked off the playground to learn anger management and not promoted to any position of leadership.

People who make themselves matter continually lift another up and encourage them to be more than they can imagine themselves to be.

- Carl Youngberg

It is interesting to note that an issue in many of my coaching assignments has revolved around workplace bullying and anger.

In the workplace today, a boss's inability to control his or her emotional behavior is just an employee complaint waiting to be filed.

In one of my seminars about attitude, the foundational work is really about Emotional Intelligence or EQ. The definition of EQ is our ability to manage our own emotions. Where IQ measures intellectual capacity, EQ looks at the ability to understand self and effectively work with themselves and others.

The difference between a successful person and others is not a lack of strength, not a lack of knowledge, but rather a lack of will.

- Vince Lombardi

People are dynamic and the knowledge that we can truly change and grow using our own potential is determined by self awareness and willingness to take a hard look at ourselves.

Check your attitude at the door.

Carl's Final Word

Attitude is the pathway between our intentions and our actions. If your outcomes are not what you desire, be willing to check your attitude

Attitude.

Put your knowledge to work.

Practical Applications.

#6
Humility.

Humble Leaders - An Oxymoron?

Humility is often misunderstood in our culture where it seems to be confused with humiliation. In fact, it seems much of the humor of sitcoms is focused on humiliating a character.

I see humility as the state of being humble. In the business world, I often hear the quality of humility attributed to a co-worker who puts others first.

There are some who say humility is not a strong business trait, as if saying "please" is a quality that would make your business request less strong to others. Yet, see what employees want and need at work to perform at their best. In a worldwide survey by **Rob LeBow** in his book, *"A Journey Into the Heroic Environment,"* see what was at the top of their list of eight employee must-haves:

- To be given credit when it's due
- To work for an honest, ethical organization
- To be a part of an environment where people put others' interests ahead of their own

All of these points are elements of living humbly and go to the heart of humility in the workplace. But when I ask workshop participants to point out others who they see practicing humility, there are never more than a few.

Sherron Watkins, the Enron whistle-blower, in an interview (*Time Magazine*, June 5, 2006) wonders if we recognize and value the appropriate traits in our leaders. As she puts it: "We want honest leaders, who are decisive, creative, optimistic and even courageous, but we so easily settle for talk that marks those traits instead of action. Worse, we often don't even look for one of the most critical traits of a leader: humility. A humble leader listens to others. He or she values input from employees and is ready to hear the truth, even if it's bad news. Humility is marked by an ability to admit mistakes."

What does humility mean to you?

In a leader, this quality is seen as priceless but rare. A humble person is generally thought to be unpretentious and modest with strong integrity: someone who does not think he or she is better or more important than others. Frank Lloyd Wright said famously, "What is needed most in architecture today is the very thing that is needed most in life – Integrity." And, humility, I might add.

Humility is not thinking less of yourself, but thinking of yourself less.

- Anonymous

Humility is humanness

I have never seen humility taught in management courses or many leadership courses, for the joke would be who would teach it?

You can understand why. Organizations want their leaders to be visionary, authoritative, capable and motivational. Nowhere does it say anything about being **humble**.

Still, successful leaders understand that a sense of humility is essential to winning hearts and minds and to do better business. The practice of humility is an outward demonstration of our inward concern and compassion, as well as being authentic in our dealings.

Humility Checkpoints:

There are three core business behaviors that can be barriers to humility. See if they sound familiar.

1. **Winner takes all**. Humility is probably the most difficult virtue to achieve, mostly because egotistic pride works so much better than humility in a competitive society. Think of all the star players in the NFL; how many really stand out as a good role model of personal humility? Then think about your own company. Are the results any better?

2. **The Star**. Feeling good about your business success can easily lapse into pride, especially when others heap praises on you. Pride sneaks in and your head begins to swell so big you could star as a float in the Macy's Thanksgiving Day Parade. How does your organization recognize success?

3. **Self focus**. Humility thrives only when your attention is directed away from yourself and towards serving others. It withers away whenever attention is directed toward its presence. When the big prize is achieved in business, is the team the thing?

   - Carl Youngberg, on leadership in the workplace

In the concept of leader/follower, leaders who are followed must be leaders who understand the human condition, especially their own.

Those in authority who are blind to their inner-selves are likely to do stupid things, such as invading other countries. Freud said, "If you don't do your inner work, your inner work will do you."

In the Tom Hanks movie *Cast Away*, our worst fears become real as he is marooned on a desert island. As portrayed by Hanks, an anal-retentive productivity expert in the film, he comes to realize much about himself and life choices he could make. His island life was actually a journey in humility and willingness and, when he returned home he was a changed man.

Humility
- a strange thing. The minute you think you've got it, you've lost it.

~

Is the development of humility a slow process or a quick jab in the ribs? Read this anonymous story of another shipwreck survivor:

> The survivor was washed up on a small, uninhabited island. He prayed feverishly for God to rescue him, and every day he scanned the horizon for help, but none seemed forthcoming.
>
> Exhausted, he eventually managed to build a little hut out of driftwood to protect himself from the elements and to store his few possessions.
>
> One day, after scavenging for food, he arrived home to find his little hut in flames, with smoke rolling up to the sky. The worst had happened, and everything was lost. He was stunned with disbelief, grief and anger.
>
> "God, how could you do this to me?" he cried.
>
> Early the next day he was awakened by the sound of a ship that was approaching the island. It had come to rescue him.
>
> "How did you know I was here?" the weary man asked his rescuers.
>
> "We saw your smoke signal," they replied.

As our shipwreck survivor discovered, he had to lose everything to be found. When money, title or possessions are the basis for our self image, humility cannot co-exist.

Early Americans found that watercress was a good indicator of the purity of the water in springs they would encounter. It will only grow where the water is pure.

Just so is humility. It will only grow and flourish in pure conditions.

Humility is not to be confused with humiliation, which is the act of making someone else feel ashamed and is something completely different.

A psychologist friend tells the story of going to his young son's first karate match. As the boys dressed in their outfits and faced each other across the mat and bowed, his son began to berate his opponent.

In a steady stream of abuse, the boy continued to put down his match mate.

The father sat stunned in the stands. He couldn't believe what was happening.

After the match, my friend pulled his child aside and said, "Son, what in the world were you doing? Why were you saying all those things?"

His son replied, "Before you begin your match, you are supposed to humiliate your opponent."

Ah ha! My friend then had to explain the difference between practicing humility versus practicing humiliation.

Because the quality of humility is rare, it becomes very important when you encounter it in co-workers. People who make themselves matter want to investigate and own this wonderful ability.

While "acting as if" is a great way to add any of these 10 simple truth qualities, be aware of the price of false humility.

A revealing old Jewish joke shows the other side of humility. In the village synagogue, during the High Holy Days, the rabbi prostrates himself on the floor, saying, "God, before You I am nothing." Immediately the richest man in town prostrates himself on the floor, saying, "God, before You I am nothing." Right after that the town beggar prostrates himself on the floor, saying, "God, before You I am nothing."

The rich man whispers to the rabbi "Look who thinks he's nothing."

In the line written by William Shakespeare, he says, "I thank my God for my humility." This statement sounds like the right way to affirm yourself in your humility. But it is actually a paradox because those who really seek and practice humility focus not on self but on others.

> *The legacy of heroes is the memory of a great name and the inheritance of a great example.*
>
> **- Benjamin Disraeli, Prime Minister of Great Britain**

Is there a business case for humility in management and leadership? In his book, *Good to Great*, **Jim Collins** seems to think so. He considers humility to be a key quality in Level 5 companies. Level 5 refers to the highest level in a hierarchy of executive capabilities, according to Collins.

Collins reported the results of a five-year study of companies that made the leap from being good and competent to greatness. Among other things, great companies are able to demonstrate sustained outstanding performance for 15 years.

If we only have great companies, we will merely have a prosperous society, not a great one. Economic growth and power are the means, not the definition, of a great nation.

- Jim Collins

Transformation to greatness is possible when leaders are able to combine extreme personal humility with intense professional will. What should good companies do to join the ranks of such elite, great companies as Coca-Cola and Intel? Look at the leaders.

Jim Collins says the characteristics common to these leaders of great organizations include:

- A discernable sense of personal humility
- Professional will and clarity of purpose
- Unwavering resolve to finish
- The practice of giving credit to others while assigning blame to themselves.

In the JimCollins.com Web discussions, Collins asks, "Which is harder to cultivate within yourself: Humility or will?"

He concludes that qualities of this leadership style allow people to:

- Avoid drawing attention to themselves
- Quietly focus their energy on building a great company
- Reflect a study in duality: modest and willful, shy and fearless

The true measure of a man is how he treats someone who can do him absolutely no good.

- Dr. Samuel Johnson

An old tool used in the recruitment and hiring business is to watch how applicants, especially at senior levels, behave when they go to lunch or dinner as part of the recruitment process.

While personal etiquette is of importance (you use silverware from the outside placement ending next to the plate), more important is how the person interacts with the service personnel. Not just the coat check but throughout the meal. Candidates who are considerate of those who help and serve them are leaders who will probably build a team of loyal and considerate executives who can still be highly competitive and resourceful.

Humility is one of the top leadership qualities that make your organization matter.

The simple truth about humility is that living simply and with humility is a way of life.

Carl's Final Word

Humility is alive and well around us.
It does not boast, it has to be discovered.
Can you quickly name five people in your life
who practice humility?

Humility.

Put your knowledge to work.

Practical applications.

#5
Someday is NOT a day of the week.

The Army says, "Be, Know, Do."
Ultimately, you have to "Do."

      - Carl Youngberg

Do, or do not. There is no try.

      - Yoda

To do is to be **- Nietzsche**

To be is to do **- Kant**

Do be do be do **- Frank Sinatra**

What I relearned back in kindergarten

It was development day at the pre-school. Gathered in the large activity room were a group of young mothers of pre-schoolers.

My purpose in speaking at the gathering was to network their shared visions and personal missions around their families.

Most were now stay-at-home moms and had felt anxiety about the workplace moving on without them and anxiety about their new role as both moms and former workers.

If there is one thing I have learned from all my running, it is that as long as you keep putting one foot in front of the other, the scenery will change over time and so will your attitude and outlook. ....Run On!!

- Dan Janick, marathon runner

My talk that day was based on the topics in the book, *Who Moved My Cheese*.

It is the story of two little people and two little mice who live in a maze and try to find an unending source for their cheese. Along the way, they deal with fears, anxiety, indecision and the usual things that fill our lives today.

But the big question that fills the majority of the session is "What would you do if you weren't afraid?" The responses are always insightful and revealing which is what makes the program so valuable.

Take a risk. Make a decision. Pay the price.

- Helen Manic, professor

I divided the group into smaller sections so participants could discuss the question and come up with their answers. When they reconvened, attendees shared what they had learned in their dialogues.

As they spoke, I heard a recurrent theme of how "someday" they wanted to get back to their writing and to their art or other pursuits. "Someday" would see them reengaged in their particular passion.

Do you have hope or a plan?

As they shared, my mind began to comprehend the impact of all these delayed objectives. I asked the participants to pause for a minute as I restated what they had been saying. I began to speak:

> Each of you has a child or children. Most of you have spouse or partner requirements. Most of you had responsible jobs or work you did before your

children arrived. Now you make a home for your family.

One of the challenges you face is the tyranny of the urgent. A child calls your name. The phone rings. Emails sit unanswered begging to be answered.

Yet each of you has a rich source of creativity, of productivity, of mature thinking and, yes, experience within you. Where do you find the balance that lets you know what matters most?

When I hear your chorus of 'somedays,' I have to consider what you are really saying. Do you have hope or a plan? Don't confuse them.

In my coaching work, I often hear **wishes dressed up like strategies.** In those experiences and in what you have shared today, **I would say that 'someday' is not a day of the week.**

With those comments, the moms in the room picked up their pens and began to write. I was perplexed. Finally, I asked what they were doing. Their answer was that they were writing down what I just said.

"What did I say," I asked.

"Someday is not a day of the week," they responded.

As I thought about their comment, it occurred to me that it was a fairly astute observation.

I then asked them for paper and pen and wrote it down for myself, and now it is one of my 10 Simple Truths. Sweet.

But the story doesn't end here. A month later, I got an email.

In it, two of the women who had talked about pursing their art and writing skills made the decision to meet each week at Starbucks for an accountability session.

Because of their appreciation of our session together, they had written the following poem about finding and living their passion.

I dedicate Simple Truth # 5 to these brave women who speak to many of us.

Bon Appetit

Happiness is my cheese
The fabulous desert of life
As a nice camembert with raspberries
Or imported Swiss fondue

Searching for it everywhere
Scamper through the maze
Opportunities to savor the cheese
A brilliant presentation

Misplaced sometimes or overlooked
Even as it stands
As big as day in front of me
I scurry somewhere else

Who took the cheese? It's disappeared
A thief extraordinaire
Accusing others of the crime
When I stole it from myself

"Just Do It" – is related to "Someday is not a day of the week."

What is the power of **Just Do It**? This Nike slogan has become one the top five slogans of the 20th century and often used throughout our language. It is a strong call-to-action slogan.

Analysis Paralysis

Bob C in an on-line blog dialogue recently discussed the power of "JUST DO IT" and its call-to-action message.

He said, "I figured out that you can't really sit and think yourself out of something. Over-thinking is quite a nifty trick that you can play on yourself. It tricks you into believing that you are on your way to solve your problem. It keeps you protected against perceived dangers out there in the world like failure, rejection and embarrassment by keeping your actions to a minimum. It feeds your ego and tells you that you know more than others, that you are a clever person that has things figured out."

When you know better, you do better.

- Oprah Winfrey

Bob on his blog has figured out that the bottom line in "someday" is a lie we tell ourselves. Over-thinking is our way of saying - not yet.

At a certain point, I just felt, you know, God is not looking for alms, God is looking for action.

- Bono

For Thomas A. Edison, action, any action, was part of his process. "Just because something doesn't do what you planned it to do doesn't mean it's useless." His statement resonates because Edison, the inventor, made countless tries before perfecting the light bulb design. He "discovered" each time he performed another test.

If you believe that someday it's going to happen, some day it probably will happen. You just have to make sure you're there when it's happening, and ideally you're at the front of the parade, and the principle beneficiary of when it happens, but it's not a kind of thing where you just sort of sit back and wait.

- Steve Case

The practice that scientists use of testing and retesting is far more applicable than to be only reserved for inventor types. I love to cook, and the physics of food never fails to amaze me. Little additions of spices or foods radically alter the taste and appearance of my meals. My approach also means that many dishes I prepare come out different each time.

Lots of people know what to do, but few people actually do what they know. Knowing is not enough! You must take action.

- Anthony Robbins

My business team-building cooking sessions called **Free Range Team Cuisine** is full of those kinds of points exactly. If you want to learn a lot about your co-workers, get them all in one kitchen and start cooking.

Do different results mean I cannot eat the results? Hardly. A recipe can be a only starting point or how exactly it should be prepared.

The choice is yours. Just do it.
Come out of life's waiting room
and seize your someday.

Carl's Final Word

When I was a small boy, I shook the hand of President Harry S. Truman. While never slick, he was savvy. His quote, "If you can't stand the heat, stay out of the kitchen" is a marvelous comment that speaks to the "someday" dreamers. Come on in the kitchen—good things are always cooking.

Someday is NOT a day of the week.

Put your knowledge to work.

Practical Applications.

#4

Be willing to make mistakes.

Experience is a bunch of mistakes – my mistakes.

      - Carl Youngberg

Have you ever made a mistake? I have and I am glad I have. Some of my greatest learnings have come from the mistakes I have made.

In fact, as a speaker and an executive coach, I turn those mistakes into experience, and I sell that experience in my work. And you can too.

I see the resistance to making mistakes in our work. If we are in an environment in which the boss's job is to "catch" us making a mistake, then mistakes grease the chutes out the door.

But I heard one of the most successful property owners in town recently tell his property purchasing group that he wanted them to make more mistakes.

More mistakes? He wanted his team to see what could be learned from any errors that strategic risk-taking could provide.

What a wise man he is to embrace the need to grow and stretch in what we do, knowing that not everything works out but the learning remains.

I can accept failure. Everyone fails at something. But I can't accept not trying.

- Martin Luther King, Jr.

My favorite "mistake" happened when I was Director of Epicure at Neiman Marcus.

As Chef Carl, we had come up with a great idea--a Neiman Marcus Gourmet Trash Bag. The bags were a vibrant red with the strong NM logo across each bag.

A true fashion statement in trash

Down in Public Relations, my colleague **Pat Zajac** and I labored over the press release that would tell everyone of these wonderful new additions to the world economy.

We included every trite and corny line we could about status trash bags including lines such as:

- Bags for the better class of trash
- Dress up your curb and your neighborhood
- A fashion statement in trash
- The perfect "His and Hers" holiday gift

We were busy gathering our witty sayings into the press release. Later, we swore we were not drinking as we wrote it.

It must have been the slowest news day in history. I think nothing newsworthy happened to anyone that day all over the world. Our press release got picked up by every news organization in the land. The release was accompanied by a picture of an English butler in a livery coat daintily dropping the bag at the curb in front a stately Dallas mansion.

Our upscale trash bags were perfect and the customers loved them. They were the fashion fad of that season—I think the pet rock fad of the 70's was a similar but grander phenomenon. Customers gave the bags as gifts, and the bags themselves were used as gift wrap for large items, which wasn't such a bad idea.

We were briskly selling out when something went terribly, terribly wrong.

The good trash haulers of San Diego decided they would NOT pick up these bags because they were the same red color as toxic waste bags. Oops! I even made *Time Magazine* with this one.

In the annals of business mistakes, my boo-boo doesn't even warrant a footnote. No one was forced out or fired as a result. The error really didn't affect the bottom line as we had sold out anyway.

Lessons from the Trash

What I learned from this misstep was not about producing Neiman Marcus trash bags. I am glad I did and would do so again with the right opportunity.

The mistake was in not involving others in the bag design process. One quick word from the right source would have gotten us a similar design or color that would fly also off the shelves and off the curb. The mistake was in not taking advantage of the team knowledge to make better decisions in the design.

It was a relatively small mistake and easily avoidable the next time. It's the kind of mistake that we make all of the time. Why is it important?

When written in Chinese, the word 'crisis' is composed of two characters. One represents danger. The other represents opportunity.

- John F. Kennedy

To be honest, more of us are making bigger decisions in less time--and with less information--than we ever have before. The buffer of enough time and enough staff to talk out every decision has almost disappeared. That's why, almost out of necessity, we are messing up more than ever. The flip side of making progress is making mistakes.

"If you're not making mistakes, you're not taking risks, and that means you're not going anywhere," said **John W. Holt Jr.**, co-author of *Celebrate Your Mistakes*. "The key is to make errors faster than the competition, so you have more chances to learn and win."

Fred Gleeck, the selling process speaker and author, has this disclaimer in his online e-zine, "If you find typographical or grammatical errors in this email, they're here for a purpose. Some people actually enjoy looking for them, and we strive to please as many people as possible."

I would love to ask **Jack Welch** about the positives of making mistakes. He was featured in a recent newspaper interview talking about his life managing teams at GE.

The biggest kick in running a big company like GE was seeing all the others who worked there become successful. People used to say what a marvelous job I did running GE. It's almost ludicrous on its face to think I could run GE. If you don't have a team of great smart people around you, you don't have a chance.

- Jack Welch, former CEO GE

I believe Jack and his team made some mistakes and probably learned from them.

Build a new box

Great leaders know the need for reaching outside the box, and when they do, the box can fall. **Vernon Sanders Law**, a retired Major League Baseball pitcher, said, "Experience is a hard teacher because she gives the test first, the lesson afterwards."

Growing up on a farm in Missouri, my life was filled with old farmers who talked a lot. My favorite quote was the oft repeated *"if it ain't broke, don't break it."*

I heard it so often, I thought it was true.

It ain't true.

Right now, there are people and organizations around the world working on ways to do our jobs cheaper and faster than we can do our jobs. **Thomas Reeder**, database entrepreneur and friend, reminds me our best customer is our competition's prime prospect. Our competitors are constantly "breaking it" to see how they can do it better.

America's call to action is to take a hard look at everything we do or someone else will. For a long time, this country rested comfortably on the shoulders of our natural resources and used them so freely and without restraint that our waterways have become unsuitable for their primary function of providing us clear, clean drinking water.

The cattle industry has been one of our core strengths and the basis of much of national identity. However, the cattle factories blemished the soil around them with waste and runoff, abusing our agrarian heritage.

Our manufacturing strength of mechanized factories (think WWII) has been deemed old economy and is quickly evaporating from our land and moving to foreign shores. Now we depend exclusively on our intellectual powers and creativity for our future success.

> *To live a creative life, we must lose our fear of being wrong.*
>
> **- Joseph Chilton Pearce**

I've been to India and saw a whole lot of very bright people studying how to get ahead of the competition--us. They can be a great resource for us but only if we know how to partner with them.

There is a lot of discussion on this topic sparked by **Thomas Friedman's** book *The World is Flat,* a synopsis and analysis on globalization.

In talking about the new world economy and what it really means to average people, an Episcopal priest-friend wants to write a book entitled, *The world is flat - again.* To succeed today is to shake up the status quo to see who remains standing and what gets broken.

In the classic movie, *The Graduate*, the wise counsel of the day to new graduates was to embrace "plastics" as the wave of the future. The advice was to get a job with plastics. What is the "wise counsel" for today?

What will you do with it?

My advice is to take what ain't broken and break it - now.

Carl's Final Word

Stanley Marcus said, "The road to success is paved with failures...handled well." To not make a mistake is to not live. It is what you do with the results of the mistake that will distinguish you in the field and serve to make yourself matter to others.

Or as Frank Wilczek, American theoretical physicist and Nobel laureate said, "If you don't make mistakes, you're not working on hard enough problems. And that's a big mistake."

Be willing to make mistakes.

Put your knowledge to work.

Practical applications.

#3

Believe that you can achieve it. Our beliefs empower us to achieve what we conceive.

Eighty percent of success is showing up.

- Woody Allen

Believe: to have confidence in the truth, the existence, or the reliability of something, although without absolute proof that one is right in doing so: Only if one believes in something can one act purposefully."

- Random House Dictionary

What do you believe in?
What does your organization believe in?

I ask participants in my keynotes and workshops these two questions. First, what answers am I seeking? Certainly not the recitation of the mission, vision and values statements hung on the wall in dusty picture frames.

I simply want to know if you believe in your company. If you do, then no one else's opinion can sway you.

And, secondly, does your company believe in you? Is there evidence to support that belief?

When you join a company, you become part of their ideology, a belief system. I am fortunate in that both of my long-term employers (Saks Fifth Avenue and Neiman Marcus) had beliefs in how they operated their businesses that meshed with mine. Beyond the flash and the glitter of the stores was a belief system in both their employees and their customers that was very appealing to me. When Stanley Marcus said, "If it's not good for the customer, then it's not good for Neiman Marcus," I felt our belief systems were aligned.

I don't think we start to believe until we have to or we are pushed because there is no other option. Whether in reaching a sales goal, raising productivity, or tackling a common issue such as reducing customer processing time or hospital infections do we make the *"believe"* choice and take action.

I have worked with people who worked for a company for years and complain and whine about it the whole time. If you don't believe in a certain practice of your business, seek to change it. If change is in not in the cards, leave.

If you don't believe in the philosophy of the company, seek change. If the company won't change, leave the company.

It is so important to believe in the work you do and the people you work with. This is truly the foundation for the shared mission of the organization, be it selling tires at the best price and have them installed in a short period of time or building a global organization that believes in the services and products you provide.

Business writer **Stevie Ray** writes in the *Minneapolis Business Journal* about the importance of business belief. "You owe it to yourself and everyone you work and live with to believe that your company's philosophy and doctrine are the best. And not just the parts that suit you or that are comfortable. As in things spiritual, only your true belief will inspire you to business success."

The doyenne of door-to-door beauty, **Mary Kay Ash** operated with a system of core beliefs that lifted her along the path to fame and wealth. "Don't limit yourself. Many people limit themselves to what they think they can do. You can go as far as your mind lets you. What you believe, remember, you can achieve."

Go climb a mountain – and believe

Arlene Blum believes. She has been to paradise and back having made more than 300 successful ascents, including the first all-woman climb to the top of Denali, the American Bicentennial Everest Expedition, as well as a 2,400-mile trek across Bhutan, Nepal, and India. She led the first all-woman expedition up the treacherous slopes of Annapurna (in Nepal) the world's 11th highest peak. She chronicled the expedition in her documentary, *Annapurna: A Woman's Place* and in her book of the same name. She stands as a model of pioneering leadership.

Now Arlene, who conducts seminars on leadership for organizations, tells what separates people who make it to the top from those who don't. "The real dividing line is passion," says Blum. "As long as you believe that what you're doing is meaningful, you can cut through fear and exhaustion and take the next step."

The fateful five percent is the hardest part --and the most important

"In so many of the things we do in life--from projects at work to household chores to climbing a mountain--we find reasons not to do the last five percent. With a Himalayan expedition, you spend years raising funds, you travel all the way to Nepal, you carry loads between camps for six weeks. Then, finally, it's summit day and you're hours from the top--but it's too cold, it's too steep or you're too tired.

"I've been so successful in my climbing because I usually haven't turned back during that final, exhausting five percent. Making it to the top isn't about a final sprint; it's about maintaining your rhythm--even if that rhythm is five breaths for every one step. That kind of focus means that you're more likely to have the energy to deal with unforeseen challenges--and less likely to lose sight of why you're climbing the mountain in the first place."

My friend, **Hank Hunt**, tells the story of the old monk who remarked once that he could learn more by climbing one mountain 500 times than he could by climbing 500 different mountains.

Like the boxer Rocky Balboa, we, as a business team, must believe we can overcome whatever obstacles are ahead before we take action.

They say there is no God in Hollywood, but I say there couldn't be a film produced if it didn't ultimately have belief as part of its story line. We want to believe.

> *College totally changed my life. It changed what I believe and what I think about everything. I majored in philosophy.*
>
> **- Steve Martin**

Ralph Hodgson, the English poet, had a great vision when he said, "Some things have to be believed to be seen." Do we hold off on total commitment until we see convincing evidence? That is often our undoing.

Only recently have we begun to believe in things that have not happened or we have not seen. To showcase that behavior, I often use Hollywood DVDs to highlight differing behavioral styles. For years, the only male leadership behavior found in movies was the John Wayne type of "jump in with both barrels." But now, change is afoot.

The plot for the blockbuster film, *Independence Day,* in which aliens attack the world is that man's best weapon is the will to survive.

That's a big challenge but we are up to it. When I asked a recent gathering who saved the world in the film, the response was **"Will Smith."** His rambunctious fighter pilot behavior is a style we are accustomed to, but there is a new fighter in town that actually does save the world.

That is David Levinson, an ex-scientist turned cable technician, played by **Jeff Goldblum.** Jeff figures out the weak point in the alien spaceship and devises the plan to accomplish its destruction.

I have not given away too much of the plot for there actually is no more plot than this.

What is interesting to us is the audience's "belief" that a nerdy cable technician, formerly gawked at and jeered in high school, now is cheered as a hero. We see the same high-tech hero in the movie *Flight of the Phoenix* and *Contact* with **Jody Foster.** Now we often call these folks "boss" in our high tech world. Go figure.

Watch your thoughts; they become words.
Watch your words; they become actions.
Watch your actions; they become habits.
Watch your habits; they become character.
Watch your character; it becomes your destiny.

- Frank Outlaw

Engage -- to get engaged

Make Yourself Matter people are actively engaged employees who consistently exert high levels of discretionary effort and outperform disengaged employees across numerous dimensions, e.g., productivity, attention to detail, teamwork and initiative.

Compared to engaged employees, disengaged employees not only do less work and work less productively, they cost their company money through twice as many missed days and dramatically higher rates of turnover.

Furthermore, since disengaged employees are also most likely to be the poorest performing employees, they require more resources in terms of time and attention from their supervisor and human resources.

How do you build *Make Yourself Matter* work teams of engaged employees who believe they can achieve what they conceive?

Too often, we think of our jobs and our careers as being the same thing. They're not. Jobs are given and jobs are taken away -- often by forces you can't control. But your career belongs to you. You get to decide everything about it: where you go, what you do, whom you work with. Don't hesitate to spend real time -- six months, a year -- figuring out your career trajectory. It's the best investment you'll ever make.

- Katharine Mieszkowski, Senior Writer- Fast Company

In general, corporate leaders and human resource professionals have sought to increase employee productivity by motivating their workforce with reward and recognition programs.

The vast majority of these programs have been ineffective in promoting sustained levels of employee productivity because motivating employees and engaging employees require very different approaches.

Traditional reward and recognition programs lack "staying power" because, like diets, they are narrowly focused on clearly identified goals as opposed to changing habits and core underlying beliefs.

Instead of "losing weight," the preference would be to "live a healthy lifestyle." Business leaders who wish to foster corporate vitality must focus on engaging--not motivating--their workforce.

It's old thinking to imagine that you can hold on to a business model and outsmart the consumer. You can't.

- Lorraine Bolsinger, VP ecomagination

Living a life that matters doesn't happen by accident. It's not a matter of circumstance but of choice.

Choose to live a life that matters.

Carl's Final Word

Great people believe. Without that belief structure, the Phoenix would never have had its movie flight, and Apollo 14 would have never occurred.

Instead of the messages of scarcity from our childhoods, Stephen Covey challenges us to believe in abundance which is a leap of faith for each of us.

Believe you can achieve it.
Our beliefs empower us to achieve
what we conceive.

Put your knowledge to work.

Practical applications.

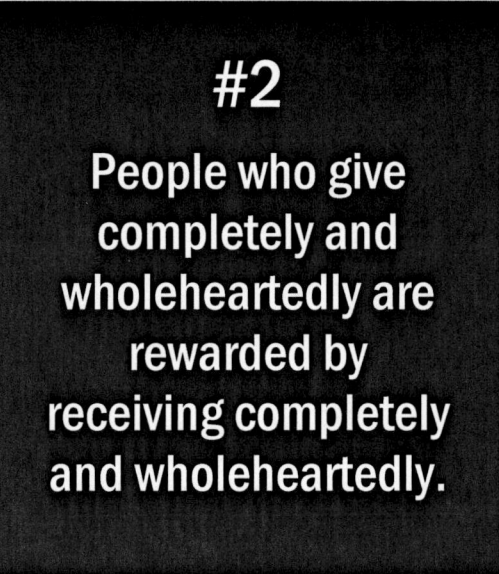

#2

People who give completely and wholeheartedly are rewarded by receiving completely and wholeheartedly.

Live Generously

Several years ago, on one of my annual mission trips to Honduras, I was in a small school in a mountain village and saw a young girl of probably 11 years of age reading one of the books we had brought to start a library for them.

It was a book on ballet and beautifully illustrated in lush watercolors. As I watched the young girl carefully turn the pages, several thoughts filled my head.

One thought was that she would probably live her life without ever seeing a ballet.

And two, she might never get to see herself be beautiful.

Life in Honduras is rough, and young people age quickly -- with hard work and early families.

Tutu time

Two years later, as I was preparing to return to Honduras, I was at a pre-departure dinner for the missioners. As we sat after dinner, I had an idea of organizing some ballet classes for students. I asked **Lynn Bissett**, the education leader of the mission trip, whether they could make such a thing happen. They assured me they could.

Here is where the giving begins. My call to the executive director of the local ballet organization asking for costumes elicited his response, "How many would you like and when would you like them?"

A call to other organizations received the same positive response. A newspaper article on the effort generated more generous giving. The teenage daughter of spin class friends told her parents she wanted to donate her recital costumes. (Note: many girls hang on to these for dress up for their own future children)

All in all, boxes of tutus, dance tights, colorful costumes, ballet CDs and more arrived which made for colorful luggage for me when I arrived in Honduras.

Then the dance lessons began for both the girls and the boys. The Chinese dance from the Nutcracker became their debut number, and, finally, on Friday, day five of their instant ballet lessons, it was celebration day and performance time.

Though a rainy and overcast day, miraculously the sun broke through just as the celebration began. After several other acts, it was tutu time.

The girls had just received their costumes that morning and were glorious in color and in their beauty. Then, Tchaikovsky's music began, and the young beauties paraded onto the playground. With a backdrop of high mountain peaks, blue skies and brilliant sunshine pouring down, they began their dance.

At first, I like everyone else, was mesmerized by their performance. But then, I turned around and I watched the parents watching their own daughters. And there was the real performance.

Receive wholeheartedly

In their eyes and on their faces, I saw their pride and joy in seeing their children perform. And I saw something else. I saw hope.....the beginning of belief that their daughters and sons could have a life that was different than their own. They could have a life with more choices and options.

Later, a long-time mission-trip friend made the comment to me that our day of celebration may have made the biggest long-term impact on the village, because it brought a message of hope and possibilities.

Clearly, this story was not about me. I just asked folks for help. But, the simple truth that people who give completely and wholeheartedly are rewarded by receiving completely and wholeheartedly is true. I will never forget the thrill of standing on that playground, hearing the music, seeing the dancing and looking into the eyes of the parents.

What do you believe?

When you read such a concept as give wholeheartedly and ye shall receive, what comes to mind? Sunday school quotes or Aunt Helen's homilies? For many of us, spiritual quotes seem very far removed from the lives we lead.

Yet, the numbers of people I meet who are trying to change their way of living to reflect this giving mentality is amazing. When asked why, they usually respond that they have tried living the other way and it didn't work. The number one objective from my seminar attendees is often to eliminate their credit card debt and live easier. But along the way to debt reduction, they have discovered the joys of giving.

Is this a blip or a movement? I suspect it's probably both and both are embraced by our young professionals.

I see it in the "living simply" movement with its strong values. The Gen Y/ Millennials replacement squad for

Baby Boomers is quickly making its way onto the management ranks.

Eighty-million boomers will retire during the next 25 years, and there are only 46 million Gen-Xers. So Millennials will grow to dominate the workforce for the next 70 years or so.

The values of these younger workers are radically different in their expression than those of the people they are replacing. The existing incentive structure and culture often don't work for this new generation.

Balancing your life

For example, top young lawyers were once willing to sacrifice the next 10 years of their lives chained to a desk in the law library, working 100-hour weeks, for the chance to make partner. For many, this was the top of the mountain.

But increasingly, new law-school grads want work-life balance, flexible schedules and philanthropic work. They couldn't care less about partnership. The older lawyers think these younger lawyers are lazy.

I spent months on the road speaking on ethics to employees at one of the Big Three accounting firms. When the new hires and the partners were in the same room, you could see their belief structures in conflict. They may approach their Excel spread sheets the same, but their personal approaches didn't agree at all.

Don't think these new workers are going to outgrow these beliefs as was often predicted about earlier groups. If these values do not change over time, companies that want to attract, retain, manage, and motivate the next generation of workers must adapt.

One thing to remember about these newest arrivals is they are searching for authenticity in all they do. For them, they need to be involved with what matters to make themselves matter.

I never heard anything about the resolutions of the apostles, but a good deal about their acts.

- Og Mandino

What do your values reveal about your personal brand? Are you about mostly give or take? What do others think about you and the message you send?

What does giving completely look like in our business environment today? In his terrific book, *Career Warfare: 10 Rules for Building a Successful Personal Brand and Fighting to Keep It*, **David d'Alessandro** unleashes a barrage of one-line challenges to our conventional business thinking about authentic giving and receiving.

David d'Alessandro touches such sticky business issues such as the higher your profile, the more likely you will be the target for criticism and envy from colleagues. He highlights the importance of looking beyond your own navel as your world view.

d'Alessandro challenges
your business thinking

- Create goodwill outside of your own tiny kingdom

- Three powerful ways to build goodwill
  - Treat the press respectfully
  - Work very hard to make your organization successful
  - Give back

- The single most important thing you can do for your career is to lay the groundwork for an attractive, personal reputation

- Hard work and accomplishments are necessary. But they probably will not set you apart from your peers

- David d'Alessandro

As you see, this goes beyond traditional office giving. Way beyond.

Many of these thoughts were not shared by earlier generations. "Hard work is necessary but won't set us apart," says the new thinking most clearly. My grandparents who came from Sweden to work harder would shudder reading such words.

For many, finding the time to give completely and wholeheartedly seems to block us. Trying to do it all is a challenge that can wear you thin, but chucking it is unthinkable.

One legal partner, a single mom, found her way to do it all was by outsourcing her to-do list. She called a professional errand service, a group composed mostly of stay-at-home moms. Within days, she had 60 Christmas gifts ready to go, and her trusty elves had sent out more than 800 Christmas cards on her behalf.

"Some people may think that the arrangement is arrogant or impersonal," says the senior consulting partner. But her bottom line is that she outsources everyday tasks so she can focus on her work, children and community.

Who's minding the home?

I also find the person who gives completely and wholeheartedly today is not gender specific. This concept was brought home to me one day after working out at the gym. The lanky 35 year old, who had a locker next to me, played basketball twice a week at noon. As he changed into his street clothes, I noticed they were shabby at best.

Finally, I could resist no more. "Peter," I said, "I know all about casual Friday, but don't you think a torn tee-shirt, cut off shorts and ratty sandals are a bit much?"

He broke out in laughter as he told me he was a stay-at-home dad raising two young daughters. His wife is a senior executive with a global software company and travels most days of the week while he tends the home fires taking care of their girls. He plays basketball, has written a mystery novel set in corporate America and goes to Dad's Day Out at the local playground where he mixes with other dads. He is giving the gift of time to his family and is doing it wholeheartedly.

Author **Keith Ferrazzi** refers to this concept of gift of talents as "currency" and you have to "give" the currency away. He finds himself saddened by the people he meets who feel they have nothing to give away. He tells people that if you are going to build your career, or your community, or your social life, "you have to give, give, give….and not keep score."

Much of this chapter focuses on looking outside ourselves, whether practicing networking as **Dean Lindsay** shares in his book *Cracking the Networking Code* or in mentoring people within your organization to help them grow. It is *other* focused.

The focus today for Millennials is striking in its clarity about what matters most to them. Two areas jump out:

- **Civic-minded.** They were taught to think in terms of the greater good. They have a high rate of volunteerism. They expect companies to contribute to their communities—and to operate in ways that create a sustainable environment.

- **Inclusive.** Millennials are used to being organized in teams—and to making certain no one is left behind. They expect to earn a living in a workplace that is fair to all, where diversity is the norm—and they'll use their collective power if they feel someone is treated unfairly.

In today's workplace, creating community is one of the biggest challenges we have. Community breeds loyalty, communication, helpfulness, faster learning cycles, better connection with the customer and co-workers and even speeds up the sales cycle as red tape gets cut.

Building a community
where we all stakeholders

I think more than anything, building a community is critical not only for success but also for survival ... as this story illustrates:

> A mouse looked through the crack in the wall to see the farmer and his wife open a package.
>
> What food might this contain? The mouse wondered--he was devastated to discover it was a mousetrap.
>
> Retreating to the farmyard, the mouse proclaimed the warning: "There is a mousetrap in the house! There is a mousetrap in the house!"
>
> The chicken clucked and scratched, raised her head and said, "Mr. Mouse, I can tell this is a grave concern to you, but it is of no consequence to me. I cannot be bothered by it."
>
> The mouse turned to the pig and told him, "There is a mousetrap in the house! There is a mousetrap in the house!"
>
> The pig sympathized, but said, "I am so very sorry, Mr. Mouse, but there is nothing I can do about it but pray. Be assured you are in my prayers."
>
> The mouse turned to the cow and said, "There is a mousetrap in the house! There is a mousetrap in the house!"
>
> The cow said, "Wow, Mr. Mouse. I'm sorry for you, but it's no skin off my nose."

So, the mouse returned to the house, head down and dejected, to face the farmer's mousetrap alone.

That very night a sound was heard throughout the house -- like the sound of a mousetrap catching its prey.

The farmer's wife rushed to see what was caught. In the darkness, she did not see it was a venomous snake whose tail the trap had caught.

The snake bit the farmer's wife. The farmer rushed her to the hospital and she returned home with a fever.

Everyone knows you treat a fever with fresh chicken soup, so the farmer took his hatchet to the farmyard for the soup's main ingredient.

But his wife's sickness continued, so friends and neighbors came to sit with her around the clock.

To feed them, the farmer butchered the pig.

The farmer's wife did not get well; she died.

So many people came for her funeral, the farmer had the cow slaughtered to provide enough meat for all of them.

The mouse looked upon it all from his crack in the wall with great sadness.

- Anonymous

So, the next time you hear someone is facing a problem and think it doesn't concern you, remember -- when one of us is threatened, we are all at risk.

The core of *Make Yourself Matter*

I find our natural competitiveness and inclination to fix things, regardless of the true desires of others, is one of the primary enemies of coaching in the workplace. When we give to others with expectations of how the gifts should be used, we diminish the value of our gifts. Below is a story I often share with coaching clients as well as in speeches. The closing paragraph is the killer:

> A boat docked in a tiny Mexican village and an American tourist started a conversation with the fisherman. The American complimented the Mexican fisherman on the quality of his fish and asked how long it took him to catch them.
>
> "Not very long," answered the Mexican.
>
> "But then, why didn't you stay out longer and catch more?" asked the American businessman.
>
> The Mexican explained that his small catch was sufficient to meet his needs and those of his family.
>
> The American asked, "But what do you do with the rest of your time?"
>
> "I sleep late, fish a little, play with my children, and take a siesta with my wife. In the evenings, I go into the village to see my friends, have a few

drinks, play the guitar, and sing a few songs. I have a full life señor."

The American interrupted, "I have an MBA from Harvard and I can help you! You should start by fishing longer every day. You can then sell the extra fish you catch. With the extra revenue, you can buy a bigger boat."

"And after that señor?" asked the Mexican.

"With the extra money the larger boat will bring, you can buy a second one and a third one and so on until you have an entire fleet of trawlers. Instead of selling your fish to a middle man, you can then negotiate directly with the processing plants and maybe even open your own plant. You can then leave this little village and move to Mexico City, Los Angeles, or even New York City! From there you can direct your huge new enterprise."

"How long would that take?" asked the Mexican.

"Twenty, perhaps twenty-five years," replied the American.

"And after that señor?"

"Afterwards? Well my friend, that's when it gets really interesting," answered the American, laughing. "When your business gets really big, you can start selling stocks and make millions!"

"Millions? Really? And after that señor?" said the Mexican.

"After that you'll be able to retire, live in a tiny village near the coast, sleep late, play with your children, catch a few fish, take a siesta with your wife and spend your evenings drinking and enjoying your friends."

- Anonymous

For me, the lesson of this story is this: Know where you're going in life... you may already be there.

What's Given - *SHINES*

Fast Company magazine interviews business leaders during the holidays. It goes beyond "getting and having" types of questions. The magazine asks "what about giving?" They talk to leaders from a wide array of industries and backgrounds to learn how they use their time, skills and money to give something back.

Their goal is not only to identify various ways in which one person can make a difference but also to suggest that making a difference is something all of us can do. In their profiles of 17 leaders, doers and change makers, they found 17 givers who find instruction and inspiration on giving back.

A friend is someone who reaches for your hand and touches your heart.

- Anonymous

At a time of unparalleled getting and spending, they testify to the power of giving and sharing. One leader, who was born in France and came to America with only $200 in his pocket, offered this engaging thought on giving. "I've always operated on the principle that your first real dollar isn't the first dollar that you earn. Your first real dollar is the one that you give away." And if all this isn't enough to convince us to change our ways, consider a study from the *American Psychology Association*.

One of the greatest movements in my lifetime among educated people is the need to commit themselves to action. Most people are not satisfied with giving money; we also feel we need to work.

- Peter Drucker

If you shovel the snow from your neighbor's sidewalk this winter, you may be doing yourself the bigger favor, according to a study in *Psychological Science*, which suggests that giving support and assistance may be a better predictor of living longer than receiving support and assistance.

Leaders who make themselves matter are usually very aware of the necessity for high-functioning management--teams. The core of these teams is the willingness to assist others on their team whether by nature or by nurture.

The following story illustrates two teams: one fully functioning and the other on the point of extinction.

A holy man was having a conversation with the Lord one day and he said:

"Lord, I would like to know what Heaven and Hell are like."
The Lord led the holy man to two doors. He opened one of the doors and the holy man looked in. In the middle of the room was a large round table. In the middle of the table was a large pot of stew which smelled delicious and made the holy man's mouth water.

The people sitting around the table were thin and sickly. They appeared to be famished. They were holding spoons with very long handles and each found it possible to reach into the pot of stew and take a spoonful, but because the handle was longer than their arms, they could not get the spoons back into their mouths. The holy man shuddered at the sight of their misery and suffering. The Lord said, "You have seen Hell."

They went to the next room and opened the door. It was exactly the same as the first one. There was the large round table with the large pot of stew which made the holy man's mouth water. The people were equipped with the same long-handled spoons, but here the people were well nourished and plump, laughing and talking. The holy man said, "I don't understand."

"It is simple" said the Lord, "it requires but one skill. You see, they have learned to feed each other. While the greedy think only of themselves."

- Anonymous

**To get what you want,
you must help others get what they want first.**

Carl's Final Word

If you move beyond titles, job, stock values, style of living and all the trappings that surround us, we are just one beggar helping another beggar find bread.

The late Kansas City millionaire who anonymously gave $100 bills to the destitute has now been embraced and expanded by others.

A woman I know, who was going through a rough patch, was recently driving through Starbucks and found that her coffee was paid for by the driver ahead of her.

People who give completely and wholeheartedly are rewarded by receiving completely and wholeheartedly.

Put your knowledge to work.

Practical applications.

#1
Never, never, let them see you sweat.

Roseanne Rosannadanna's Prayer:

Please love down upon the Rosannadanna folks. Bring peace to our fathers, good health to our mothers, and please don't make me sweat like Dr. Joyce Brothers."

- Roseanne Rosannadanna, aka Gilda Radner

It is appropriate that this book, which began on the first page talking about fear, ends with the same topic.

Along the way, we have talked about attitude, practicing humility, making mistakes, believing, giving and now, dealing with fear. Hopefully we have found new thoughts and truths about moving fear out of our lives.

Fake it till you make it.

- Zig Ziglar

I remember the first time I was scheduled to give my first keynote speech. I was filled with terror at the prospect. I called a friend who is also a speaker and told him what I was feeling. His recipe? Turn my fear into energy!

Never, never, never, never give up.

- Winston Churchill

Pressure can play a useful role in helping us run races, knock out work at the last moment and help us address other business stress points. But stress that's powerful enough to cause fear ultimately shuts us down. Fear causes the amygdalae, regions of the brain, to release the stress chemicals cortisol and vasopressin, putting the body on alert, quickly shutting down higher-order thinking, long-term memory, and our capacity to perform.

Keeping your head above water

Mark Spitz, the famed Olympic swimmer and winner of seven Olympic gold medals in 1972, talks about fear in his book, *The Mark Spitz Complete Book of Swimming*. Mark says any fear of the water should be eliminated as soon as possible because it is the greatest handicap to learning how to swim.

Fear of the water—in very basic terms—is the fear of going under, of not being able to breathe, according to Mark. When you are afraid, your concentration is broken and your muscles are not able to work properly because you become tense. This results in impaired coordination, both in learning and in the actual physical performance. You cannot keep your body in a constant state of tension or contraction—a state that fear can cause.

We have learned in our aerobics classes that muscles can only be tensed for a limited period of time before they grow tired. They must be relaxed for them to continue functioning properly. That is why instructors rotate exercises frequently.

Fear can cause you to lose concentration so that your mind blots out all helpful incoming stimuli and you can't hear instructions properly—if at all.

It often requires more courage to dare to do right than to fear to do wrong.

- Abraham Lincoln

Fear will track you down no matter where you go. Many times when I was starting my business, Starbucks was the safe place where I could pull myself together before making a sales call. I needed to get focused to avoid any inadvertent negative sales message that customer service speaker Jane Handly expertly defines. Jane says this fear of making a sales call can produce self-defeating statements such as, *"You don't wanna buy a pencil, do ya"?*

FEAR is the acronym of "future events appearing real." What happens when we are overcome with fear? We find ourselves being changeable, fitful, maddening, restless, irritable, and discontented.

Change agents like **Paul Birch** from British Airways explains in *Fast Company* why he has to go to such lengths to persuade people to tell the truth: **fear**.

"People build up trivial things into life-threatening situations," Birch says. "You know the classic fear: I'll get sacked if I disagree with my boss or if I propose off-the-wall ideas -- even if they're good ideas."

Tackling fear head-on

Paul asks employees to list ideas they believe would get them fired. Then he works through each item on each list: "Is this really going to get you sacked?" he asks them. "If it might -- but it's the seed of a good idea -- how could you change it so that you won't get sacked?"

Fear is not the only factor that prevents honesty, Birch adds. Too many companies lack role models for candor, especially at high levels. Employees would be more honest, he believes, if senior executives talked more openly about their own failures: "It's not okay to have a track record of mistakes, but it's okay to make mistakes."

Lessons from an octopus

For those who enjoy a good Italian octopus entree, the story of how they come to your dinner plate can be a cautionary tale on making important choices.

Octopi are caught off the coast of Barcelona in small pottery pots placed on the ocean floor. With small openings compared to the body of the pots, the unsuspecting octopus will then crawl in for a restful night far from his oceanic compatriots.

When along comes the fishing boat and yanks the pot rope up, the snug octopus, obviously thinking he's still safe, stays all curled up in the pot, unaware of what is awaiting him.

To evict him, they pry him out spraying a noxious solution like bleach. This irritates the octopus so that he slithers out of the pot, right into the large basin in the boat to be transferred to the nearest restaurant and then, of course, your dinner plate.

I see parallels for all of us in the process we must go through to leave our comfortable rut and to move into the new behavior and conditions we are drawn to. The work of *Making Yourself Matter* is not easy. In fact, our very nature tells us to climb into that snug little pot and have a cup of tea.

Excuses dressed up as reasons

But we must always remember the WHY of making the move. Crawling into that pot is often second nature and certainly convention wisdom.

Past seminar participants have told me that *Make Yourself Matter* is the "spray bleach" that can jolt us out of the rut we may get in. I often quote the wise saying that the difference between a rut and a grave is just a matter of inches. We all need to get out of the "*comfort zone*" rut and into the new world.

Most of us are great scriptwriters for excuses dressed up as reasons for not tackling the issues in front of us. Those reasons can be relationships, poor job fit, more education, better boundaries, speaking up in meetings and keeping our true worth hidden, often, even to ourselves. Simple truths such as attitude and willingness to give completely can be the tools that help us focus and move past our fears.

Marcia L. Conner, former senior manager of worldwide training at Microsoft, has written insightfully about fears in the workplace. As a recognized authority on workplace learning, her insights are valuable.

The Five Fears Of Learning:

As a coach and educator, I see five fears of learning play out:

- Worry over others' opinions
- Anxiety around changing routines
- Panic over the possibility of failing
- Personal distrust around mastering a topic
- Terror facing scary situations

Each fear leads otherwise curious people to avoid exploration and to lose out on learning experiences.

- Marsha Conner

The best antiperspirant for fear is faith.

Carl's Final Word

Building a life free of fear is the goal and process behind this book. I have validated these 10 Simple Truths and can assure you that although these truths are simple, they may not be easy to follow.

The hardest challenge to overcome may be fear. The tricky thing about fear is it can dress up to look like doubt, indecision, wisdom or caution.

Peel away the layers and there is fear. Fear stops us before we begin. If you feel stuck, re-examine the five fears of learning, and see which apply to you.

Never, never, let them see you sweat.

Put your knowledge to work.

The Path to Simple Truth # 1

Practical applications.

Final Reflections

We all want to live lives that matter. Matter to our families, our friends, our companies, our communities and ultimately to ourselves.

In hundreds of my presentations on this topic, each session has generated impressive discussion on one or more of these intense simple truths.

> *Though no one can go back and make a brand new start, anyone can start from now and make a brand new ending.*
>
> - Carl Bard, Poet

Why? Because in the world in which we live, it is hard to know what is your role and what is your legacy. In jobs that make us feel vulnerable at almost any level, we naturally want to cling to truths that stand the test of time.

We are hungry for leadership that makes sense, but we also have to take our own positive, personal action

Getting on the corporate radar

A colleague of mine shared this story linking thinking and behavior together:

> An international telecommunications company was experiencing explosive growth. Because the company was hiring hundreds of people as fast as possible, they decided to take a deeper look into the hiring and induction process to find out what made people successful in the company. According to the HR staff, too many of the new hires were not a good fit for the organization, and the staff wanted to find out what they could about employee attitudes.
>
> The HR group created focus groups to get new employees to talk about their "new hire" experiences.
>
> They enticed the first group of newly hired employees into a meeting room by offering them free pizza. The new hires had all been with the company for less than six months and spoke very openly about their love of their new employer.

Still in their employee honeymoon phase, the company could do no wrong.

The second group of employees had been with the company between six months and two years. Although the environment was the same, the results were much different. As the group of 20 or so employees sat around the table eating pizza, they grouped themselves unusually. Several of the employees who were developing very good reputations sat near each other. In another area, the "high-maintenance" employees were sitting together.

The discussion started off friendly but quickly turned into a "whine" session. The high maintenance employees started complaining about processes, management, lack of access to information, systems issues, etc.

The group of "high performing" employees were silent.

The facilitator moved the discussion to the high performing group trying to determine why they weren't having the same issues.

After careful analysis, there was a clear difference between the two groups.

The high maintenance group was always waiting for something to happen. There was an excuse keeping them from being as productive or successful as they could be. Someone else has to do something or take some action.

The high performing group didn't wait on anyone. If they experienced a lack of resources, poor management or lack of information, they didn't let it get in their way of being successful. They knew what needed to be done and then did it and moved on.

The HR Director of this rapidly growing international company realized they needed to increase their pool of keepers. This is human talent who are self-starters, self-motivators and who create value to the company regardless of their circumstances or role in the organization.

Make Yourself Matter people are high performers. They start themselves, they motivate themselves and are valuable in every thing they do on the job.

As employers, which group would you pick?

Don't put your billboard in the woods

Essentially, making yourself matter is about increasing your personal brand. Just as you would not put a billboard in the woods, you would not want to hide your strengths. In the past, long-term service in an organization gave many people a chance to view your strengths and contributions.

Now, with the average time in a company being less than two years, letting others see our strengths quickly is imperative.

Where do we go from here?

To avoid this being another book on your shelf, pick one truth and share it with someone—a mentor or a trusted colleague.

But choose that mentor carefully. Find someone who listens without advice giving. Avoid both uncritical lovers and unloving critics. Talk about it in depth. And then let others know what you stand for. If you are an authority, begin to practice it.

When you share with others, you strengthen them and yourself. And when we share, we give ourselves the gift of remembering the lessons and simple truths we have learned.

And please let me know how you are doing. I want to hear how you are applying these truths in your own life.

Following the path you have uncovered in these pages will help you become emotionally wise--where you can appreciate, and even recognize, others who are also wise. Fortunately for you, you can now blow their socks off as you live the truths you've uncovered.

You were born to be an original,
Don't die a Xerox copy.

- Carl Youngberg

What mattered to Mother Teresa

This volume closes with two stories. Mother Teresa who is someone who made herself matter. Mother Teresa posted the poem below, by **Dr. Kent Keith**, on the wall of her orphanage in Calcutta. The final story in this chapter is a powerful yet anonymous story entitled *The Choice Is Yours*.

People are often unreasonable, illogical and self-centered; Forgive them anyway.

If you are kind, people may accuse you of selfish, ulterior motives; Be kind anyway.

If you are successful, you will win some false friends and some true enemies; Succeed anyway.

If you are honest and frank, people may cheat you; Be honest and frank anyway.

What you spend years building, someone could destroy overnight; Build anyway.

If you find serenity and happiness, they may be jealous; Be happy anyway.

The good you do today, people will forget tomorrow, Do good anyway.

Give the world the best you have, and it may never be enough; Give the world the best you've got ... anyway.

You see, in the final analysis, it is between you and God, it never was between you and them anyway.

- Dr. Kent Keith, writer and speaker

The choice is yours

To close, I'd like to tell a story about a young man who lived in a small town and never trusted or believed in any thing or anyone. This lack of trust is a huge barrier to making yourself matter because you have to trust and you have to believe.

> Growing up, he tested everybody and every thing, because the young man just didn't believe that people would tell the truth or act in the right ways.

> Now in this town lived an older man who everybody referred to as the wise man, because he always seemed to be able to do and know the wise thing, not the easy thing, to do. Somewhat like Yoda in Star Wars, townspeople trusted this man and went to him for counsel on what they should do.

> Because life had taught him not to trust, the young man was skeptical and decided to go to the man's home and test him.

> He would have a small sparrow in his hand and ask this wise man if this sparrow was alive or dead. If the man said the sparrow was dead, he was going to snap the head of the sparrow and throw it to the ground.

> But if he said the sparrow was alive, he would toss it up in the air and let it fly away.

"Let's just see how wise this old man is." Off he went to the home of the wise man and knocked on his door.

When the wise man answered, he said "what can I help you with, my son."

The young man said "I would like to see how wise you are, and I have a little test to see. In my hand, I've got a sparrow and I'd like you to tell me if it is alive or dead."

The man came out to the front porch and looked the young man right in his eyes. "Young man, the answer to that question is in your hands."

- Anonymous

For each of us, to truly make ourselves matter, the answer to our future is also in our hands.

Where we are making the wise choices and deciding what next right thing to do, with every single minute of every single day and with every single breath, we are making the decision to make ourselves matter.

The future is in your hands

The Path to Simple Truths

Reflections on *Make Yourself Matter.*

The Path to Simple Truths

Put your knowledge to work.

The Path to Simple Truths

Practical applications.

Make
Yourself
Matter™

Become Your Own Best Asset

By **Carl D. Youngberg**

Speaker, Author, Coach

We have aligned Carl Youngberg's blockbuster new book, *Make Yourself Matter – Becoming Your Own Best Asset*, with behavioral analysis and team building tools to introduce four unique, new training programs to help your organization get to the heart of your business' goals.

Whether your focus is improving work efficiencies, improving communication skills, building sales or sustaining a high performance team, we have customized programs and workshops for your business. Designed as both as a business book and workbook, the contents of *Make Yourself Matter* is focused, interactive and inspirational. When integrated with team building and behavioral analysis tools--our result is a unique process that improves efficiency and achieves high performance.

- *Develop a High Performance People*
  Based on your individual behavior. Understand how you were built and how you respond to situations around you.

- *Improve Your Customer Service Process*
  Carl's background in luxury retailing, combined with each person's individual service preference, helps you understand how to serve your customers and keep them.

- *Bridge the Gap to Your Customers*
  Increase sales effectiveness and communicate better by improving sales relationships with our individual behavior.

- *Creating a Highly Engaged Team*
  Create an engaged, collaborative team by understanding each person's natural role and team style resulting in better communication and a more effective team.

If your organization has training or development needs in any of these areas, please give us a call **214-227-9916** or email David McNair at david@expertsthatspeak.com